Girl Scout Badges and Signs

Girl Scouts of the U.S.A.
830 Third Avenue
New York, N.Y. 10022

GIRL SCOUTS OF THE U.S.A.

Mrs. Orville L. Freeman, **President**
Mrs. Frances R. Hesselbein, **National Executive Director**

Inquiries related to **Girl Scout Badges and Signs**
should be addressed to Program, Girl Scouts of the
U.S.A., 830 Third Avenue, New York, N.Y. 10022.

Contents

5 **Junior Girl Scout Insignia**
5 Badges
5 Signs
6 Junior Aide Patch
6 Bridge to Cadette Girl Scouts Patch
6 Placing Insignia on Your Uniform
6 Girl Scout Badges
7 Dabbler Badges
7 Badges with Green or
   Tan Backgrounds
8 Record of Activities
8 Badge Presentations
8 Steps You Can Take to Choose and
   Complete Badges

10 **The World of Well-Being**
11 Dabbler
13 Child Care
15 Community Health and Safety
17 Exploring Foods
19 First Aid
21 Group Sports
23 Healthy Eating
25 Hobbies and Pets
   Pet Care
   "Making" Hobbies
   "Collecting" Hobbies
   "Doing" Hobbies
30 Home Living
32 Household Whiz

34 Individual Sports
36 Personal Health
38 Sports Sampler
40 Tending Toddlers

43 **The World of People**
44 Dabbler
46 Active Citizen
48 Around the Town
50 Girl Scouting Everywhere
52 Hands Around the World
54 Junior Citizen
56 Local Lore
58 My Community
60 My Heritage
62 On My Way
64 Peoples of the United States
66 The World in My Community
68 Traveler
70 Wide World
72 World Neighbors

74 **The World of Today and Tomorrow**
75 Dabbler
78 Aerospace
80 Business-Wise
82 Computer Fun
85 Do-It-Yourself
87 Energy Saver
90 Food Raiser

92   Foods, Fibers, and Farming
94   Math Whiz
96   Ms. Fix-It
98   Putting Things Together
101   Science Around Town
103   Science in Action
105   Science Sleuth
107   Water Wonders

110   **The World of the Arts**
111   Dabbler
114   Architecture
117   Art in the Home
120   Art in the Round
123   Art to Wear
125   Books
128   Communication Arts
131   Dance
133   Folk Arts
136   Musician
138   Music Lover
140   Popular Arts
142   Prints and Graphics
144   Textiles and Fibers
147   Theater
150   Visual Arts

153   **The World of the Out-of-Doors**
154   Dabbler
156   Bicycling
158   Boating
161   Eco-Action
163   Ecology
166   Finding Your Way
168   Foot Traveler
170   Hiker
172   Horseback Rider
174   Horse Lover
176   Outdoor Cook

178   Outdoor Fun
180   Swimming
182   Troop Camper
184   Water Fun
186   Wildlife

189   **Our Own Troop's Badge**
190   **Our Own Council's Badge**

191   **Junior Girl Scout Signs**
192   Sign of the Rainbow
195   Sign of the Sun
198   Sign of the Satellite

201   **Junior Aide Patch**
203   **Bridge to Cadette Girl Scouts Patch**

Junior Girl Scout Insignia

What do the insignia a Girl Scout wears on her uniform say about her to others? Quite a lot! They are official symbols of both your Girl Scout membership and what you've done as a Girl Scout.

Your Girl Scout pin and your World Association pin tell others that you are a member of Girl Scouts of the U.S.A., which is part of the World Association of Girl Guides and Girl Scouts. Your other official insignia tell a bit about what you've participated in or worked towards as a Girl Scout. By looking at your insignia someone can easily see what interests you have and the activities you've been a part of. They see all this, and you don't even need to say a word.

In Brownie Girl Scouts, you may have worked on Brownie Girl Scout Try-Its. As a Junior Girl Scout, you can explore even more through badges, signs, Junior Aide activities, and the Bridge to Cadette Girl Scouts patch.

Badges

There are 88 badges from which you can choose. Seventy-nine are described in this book and nine more are described in the **Junior Girl Scout Handbook.** Your Girl Scout group can even make up its own badge. Wearing a badge on your uniform tells others you have completed the required activities and are ready to share what you know about the topic. Juliette Low said that every badge you earn is related to our motto, "Be Prepared." She explained that a badge is not a reward or a medal; it is something you have done so often and so well you can teach it to someone else.

Signs

A sign is an invitation to action. There are four signs which Junior Girl Scouts can work towards: the Sign of the Rainbow, the Sign of the Sun, the Sign of the Satellite, and the Sign of the World. The first three are described in this book, while the fourth is in the **Junior Girl Scout Handbook.** Like badges, signs have required activities. For some parts of a sign, you might need to earn a badge. For other parts, you might help to carry out a project, such as doing something for your community. Each sign has its own symbol. When you complete the activities required for each sign, you can wear that insignia on your uniform sash as a reminder of your experience and accomplishments.

Junior Aide Patch

Junior Girl Scouts can also earn another insignia. It's the Junior Aide patch. When someone sees that you are wearing it, they know you have helped Brownie Girl Scouts do activities that will prepare them for Junior Girl Scouting.

Bridge to Cadette Girl Scouts Patch

During your last year as a Junior Girl Scout, you may earn your Bridge to Cadette Girl Scouts patch. It is earned by participating in special activities in which you find out what's ahead in Cadette Girl Scouting.

Placing Insignia on Your Uniform

Most insignia go on the front of your badge sash or vest. Look at the sash in the picture to see where to sew or pin on each piece of insignia. (Patches from events, camp, or special projects are sewn on the back of the sash.) You may wear your sash or vest as soon as you become a Junior Girl Scout.

Girl Scout Badges

Badge activities are a way to find out about, to try, or to practice something about the subject you have chosen. The directions for each badge will tell you which activities you need to complete in order to earn that badge.

For each badge you earn, there is a badge symbol you can wear on your uniform sash. It shows you have new knowledge and skills that you can use and share with others.

The badges in this book are grouped by Girl Scout interest worlds. You can easily tell which world a badge is in by the color of its border: World of Well-Being, red; World of People, blue; World of Today and Tomorrow, orange; World of the Arts, purple; and World of the Out-of-Doors, yellow.

The nine badges in the **Junior Girl Scout Handbook** have activities which span across several worlds of interest. They have a white background with a dark blue border which symbolizes the blue in the World Association pin. This blue color is a symbolic link to the worldwide movement of Girl Guides and Girl Scouts.

Dabbler Badges

You will notice that each world of interest has a Dabbler badge. A Dabbler badge has two activities for each badge area in that world. The Dabbler badge is a good one to choose if you are not sure which badge you might enjoy doing in a particular world and want to have a little taste of what each badge is like. Dabbler badges may be done when you are a Brownie Girl Scout working on the Bridge to Junior Girl Scouts patch, or any time when you are a Junior Girl Scout.

Badges with Green or Tan Backgrounds

In this book, you can see that some badges have green backgrounds and some have tan backgrounds. Cadette Girl Scouts may work on the badges with the tan backgrounds. Junior Girl Scouts may work on any of the badges—green, tan, or the white-background ones in the **Junior Girl Scout Handbook.** The tan badges were designed to take more planning and will most likely take more time to do than the green badges.

In any badge area you can start with either the green or the tan background, depending on what you like or are good at. For example, if you are very much interested in sculpture, you might want to try Art in the Round rather than Visual Arts. If you already know how to ride a horse, you would probably choose the Horseback Rider rather than the Horse Lover badge. If you don't know much about agriculture but would like to learn, you would start with Foods, Fibers, and Farming rather than Food Raiser.

Watch in many activities for the little word, "or." This means you have a choice in the activity of what you will do and can pick the part that is best for you. Some of the badges with the tan backgrounds have a "Write your own activity." That means you can think up your own activity to go with that badge topic. If you choose to write your own, be sure the activity will take at least three hours to complete and be fun and interesting to you.

Most often, you will work on badge activities with a small group of friends who are all interested in the same badge topic. Sometimes you will earn a badge that no one else has chosen.

Record of Activities

Keep a record of your badge work by putting your initials and the date beside each badge activity you do. Ask anyone who helped you to add her/his initials, too. If you did the activity on your own, explain to your leader what you did, so she may initial it. You may do part of a badge at camp. Or you might move to another place and another troop before you complete a badge. Therefore the record you keep in this book is important, because it will show what you have done and when you have finished a badge.

Badge Presentations

Badges are presented at a Court of Awards. Your troop may want to have a Court of Awards as soon as most of you have earned your first badges. You may also wait and have a big Court of Awards, with invited guests, when all the badges completed by the troop are presented.

Steps You Can Take to Choose and Complete Badges

1 Pick a badge topic that interests you, one you want to learn more about, or one that is new to you. If you and others in your troop have an interest the badges don't cover, you can create a new badge of your own. For "how to," see the Our Own Troop's badge, page 189.

2 Look through the badge activities to find those which interest you most.

3 Seek out others in the troop who would like to earn the same badges as those you have chosen. If no one else shares your interest, work out with your leader a way to do the badge on your own.

4 Find an adviser who will help you as you work on the badge, whether you work with a group or on your own. An adviser can be:
- [ ] your troop leader
- [ ] a parent, teacher, or senior citizen
- [ ] a Cadette or Senior Girl Scout
- [ ] someone else who knows the badge topic

5 Use a variety of ideas for completing badges. Badge activities may say, "show, describe, design, create, make, construct" or "keep a record." Here are some ways you might do these activities:
- [ ] draw a picture
- [ ] write a poem, story, or song
- [ ] make a collage or poster
- [ ] keep a journal, diary, or scrapbook
- [ ] take photographs
- [ ] prepare an exhibit
- [ ] write a newspaper article
- [ ] give a how-to demonstration
- [ ] describe in written or spoken words
- [ ] build models or dioramas
- [ ] put on a skit, pantomime, puppet show, or play
- [ ] put together magazine pictures
- [ ] make a diagram, chart, or list
- [ ] teach someone else the skill

6 Share what you have learned in your badges with anyone who is interested. Some of the badge activities state that you should share what you have found out. People to share with could include family members of any age, Girl Scouts of any age, neighbors, teachers, and friends.

7 Explore a variety of resources in completing your badges. Many badges say, "find out, look for, hunt." First you can try your **Junior Girl Scout Handbook.** Also, one or more of the people listed in number 6 (above) might help you. Many times a telephone directory or guide to newcomers in the community will give you ideas for available resources nearby. You might try one or more of the following:

- [ ] library
- [ ] museum
- [ ] historical association
- [ ] community information center
- [ ] Chamber of Commerce
- [ ] church, synagogue, or other houses of worship
- [ ] civic associations
- [ ] men's and women's clubs
- [ ] stores
- [ ] businesses
- [ ] tourist bureaus
- [ ] schools
- [ ] colleges
- [ ] local government offices
- [ ] local newspaper offices, radio stations, and television stations
- [ ] senior citizens' groups
- [ ] ethnic heritage groups
- [ ] post offices
- [ ] parks
- [ ] recreation areas
- [ ] nature centers
- [ ] social service offices
- [ ] health care facilities
- [ ] airports
- [ ] bus terminals and railway stations
- [ ] hobby groups
- [ ] fairs and festivals
- [ ] children's theater
- [ ] youth organizations
- [ ] government agencies
- [ ] farms
- [ ] ranches
- [ ] factories
- [ ] mills
- [ ] computer centers
- [ ] police or fire stations
- [ ] ambulance squads
- [ ] utility companies
- [ ] garden centers
- [ ] zoos
- [ ] aquariums
- [ ] botanical gardens
- [ ] boatyards
- [ ] seaports
- [ ] marinas
- [ ] camps

The World of
Well-Being

Dabbler

Complete one activity in each group.

A.1 Make something that shows the things you feel are special about families, the things you enjoy about a home, and/or the things you can do with members of a family.

2 Collect pictures of the important events that happen in the life of a family (births, marriages, deaths, etc.).

B.1 Make a picture alphabet chart or book, a set of sandpaper letters, or an original toy for a younger child. Use what you make with several children. Watch for and record their actions.

2 Collect many pictures of babies and very young children doing different activities. With an adult, talk about what ages the children might be and what they can do by themselves.

C.1 Make up a radio or television commercial or a magazine advertisement for a basic home first aid kit. It should tell what each item is used for.

2 Inspect your own home. Make a list of things you will check for. If you find things that are unsafe, help make a plan to correct them.

D.1 Find out about a health agency in your community that provides immunizations.
☐ Learn what they do and why immunizations are important.
☐ Find a way to tell others about this service.

2 Find a place in your community that needs to be cleaned up (a neighborhood park, street, vacant lot, etc.).
☐ With the help of others get the job done.
☐ Make and post safety rules to keep this place clean and safe.

E.1 Visit a place where food is prepared, grown, or processed. Find out how the food gets to consumers.

2 Collect or draw pictures of foods from the four food groups. Use them to make something which would tell others how to eat a balanced diet.

F.1 Take part in a day of sports activities or a sports tournament with other troops, schools, or community groups.

2 Invent a new group game. Dream up and make the equipment you will need. Decide on the rules and teach the game to a group.

G.1 As a group, pick one food from each of the four food groups.
☐ Price each item at two stores near your home.
☐ Compare your prices with three other troop members who have gone to different stores.
☐ Decide which store offers the best buy in each category.

2 Take care of your own clothes for at least two weeks.
☐ Wash them and iron if necessary.
☐ Find out how to make simple repairs, such as sewing on buttons and stitching torn seams.
☐ Repair several things of your own or for other family members.

H.1 Set up an obstacle course to test physical fitness. Include exercises or activities, such as climbing, jumping, running, and tumbling.
☐ Check the obstacle course for safety.
☐ Time yourself and others going through the obstacle course.
☐ Practice each skill until you improve your time.

2 Find out what a doctor or dentist does at a checkup.
☐ Learn what each piece of equipment she/he uses is called and what it does.
☐ Make up a skit or puppet show that will tell other children what will happen at the doctor's or dentist's office when they go for a checkup.

I.1 Plan an interesting afternoon for your own troop or another troop or group. Include a quiet and an active game, a song, a story, a skit or poem, and a nutritious snack.

2 Ask several adults or children about their hobbies. Find out about one that interests you. Do or make something related to the hobby.

My signature

Leader's signature   Date badge completed

Child Care

Complete four activities, including the one starred.

*1 Demonstrate that you know how to care for a young child by baby-sitting or helping out at home, in a nursery school, church school class, or informal play group.

2 Have each member of the troop pretend she's an adult and write a letter to a child care expert asking advice about raising children. Take turns coming up with and talking over the solutions. Check with adults to see if they agree with the solutions.

OR With others, role play a gathering of parents and/or teachers discussing what they feel are the most important things to teach their children.

3 The telling of a story in pictures — on a cave wall, on a water jug, or in a fabric pattern — has been a practice common to many cultural groups since ancient times. Make something that tells the story of what life is like for a child in your community.

4 Find out what a group of younger children enjoys and what they are able to do. With others, plan and carry out entertainment for some younger children for at least an hour. If possible, plan and serve a nutritious snack. Talk with the adult or parent responsible for the children about how successfully things went.

5 Make a "rainy day" activities box for younger children. Include supplies for at least six different types of activities. One of the activities should be one you created yourself. Give your box to a child or group of children.

6 Make a booklet or display that tells baby-sitter safety measures and information a sitter needs to know about the children she/he is responsible for watching. Include first aid tips and things to do if a child becomes ill. Share your findings with others.

7 With others, plan a way to help a group of younger children learn about safety. Discuss your plan with adults in charge of the children. Carry out your plan.

8 Select five commercially prepared baby foods. Make a note of price and ingredient listing. Learn how to prepare at least two of these foods on your own. Compare the taste and cost per serving of the homemade and the commercial foods.

My signature

Leader's signature   Date badge completed

Community Health and Safety

Complete six activities.

1 Find out about four health and safety services your community provides to protect you and others.
   - ☐ Visit one of these agencies.
   - ☐ Learn what it does and how to contact it in an emergency.

2 Survey your troop or class to find out the number and types of accidents they or people close to them have had in the last year.
   - ☐ Discover how and where these accidents have occurred most frequently.
   - ☐ Discuss ways to prevent such accidents from happening again.

3 Discuss with others the safety rules for:
   - ☐ talking to strangers
   - ☐ riding in a car, bus, train, or plane
   - ☐ crossing streets
   - ☐ disposing of waste

   Make a habit of setting a safe example.

4 Learn what steps you and others can follow when purchasing, preparing, storing, and serving food to keep it clean and healthy. Be sure to follow these steps.

5 Identify two diseases that pets and insects can carry. Find out what is being done to control them and what you can do to help.

6 Find out about one of the people whose job it is to help keep you healthy and safe. Learn about this person's daily routines, job training, duties, salary, and what she/he likes and dislikes about the work.

7 Search for sources of pollution in your community.
   - ☐ Find out how polluted water or air threatens your own health and that of your community.
   - ☐ Do something to help reduce the pollution.

8 Take a hazard hike along a bike path, foot trail, horse trail, skateboard course, or similar place.
   ☐ Identify places where you could get hurt or unsafe practices that could cause you trouble.
   ☐ Set up some way to warn others of the hazards.

9 Plan and carry out a playground project to make the playground a safer place.

My signature

Leader's signature   Date badge completed

Exploring Foods

Complete four activities.

1 Arrange to teach a younger child or small group of children some beginning steps in cooking. First, practice them yourself. Include reading the recipe, gathering the ingredients and necessary equipment, following the recipe, reading package labels, measuring dry and liquid ingredients, working safely in the kitchen, serving food attractively, and cleaning up.

2 At two different nearby stores, comparison shop for at least a dozen grocery items your family uses. Price items that are the same size and quality. Get at least two brands or types each (fresh, frozen, canned) of several products and hold a taste test. Have family or a group of friends rate the foods without telling them which brand they are tasting. Figure out the most popular. Share all your findings with troop members, their families, or other groups you feel would be interested.

OR Learn how to make several foods. Either grow something to eat in a window box or garden, learn how to bake several items without a mix, or make jams or pickles. Compare the cost and taste of what you make to similar products available in stores.

3 Plan a three-day menu for a family of five (three adults, a toddler, and a Junior Girl Scout) that is going camping. The family is very concerned about world food shortages and prefers nonmeat meals. They don't want to spend too much money. They do want meals that are nutritious, simple to prepare, and require little or no refrigeration. Make up menus for the meals they will have, including a snack each day.

4 Try four recipes, each one featuring one of the four food groups. One recipe should be from another country or culture. Serve your dishes to others.

5 Plan and serve an entire meal by yourself or with a small group. Include at least one item you have never prepared before. Plan the menu, shop for the groceries, set the table, prepare and serve the food, and clean up afterwards.

6 With others, plan and prepare the food for a large group celebration or gathering. Plan a menu that is nutritious and suited to the special occasion. Plan decorations and/or table setting that fit the occasion and the menu selected.

My signature

Leader's signature   Date badge completed

First Aid

Complete six activities, including the two starred.

1 Make a chart of all the telephone numbers you might need in case of an emergency.
   - [ ] Include your hospital emergency room, doctor, police and fire departments, ambulance service, and poison control center.
   - [ ] Post your chart by the telephone.
   - [ ] Practice making proper emergency calls, giving necessary information, and following directions given to you.

2 Demonstrate first aid for cuts, scratches, bruises, sprains, fractures, and fainting. Teach someone else how to do these skills.

*3 Demonstrate first aid for stopped breathing, severe bleeding, shock, and choking. Be sure to keep written instructions for these procedures in a safe place where you can review them often.

4 Design and assemble a first aid kit. Make a list of all the items included in this kit. Show how each item can be used.

5 Learn and practice the following fire safety skills:
   - [ ] how to treat burns or scalds
   - [ ] what to do if someone's clothes catch fire
   - [ ] how to design an evacuation plan for each room in your home or meeting place in case of fire

*6 Survey your home for poisonous substances. For example: medicines, cosmetics, cleaning solutions, and plants.
   - [ ] Be sure these substances are properly labeled and stored in a safe place out of the reach of small children.
   - [ ] Show the proper first aid for poisoning.

7 Imagine that a person has been out in the cold too long or suddenly stops breathing due to heart failure. Practice what to do if:
☐ you are giving first aid
☐ you are a bystander and someone else is giving first aid

8 Learn about the emergency disasters that could affect you, such as a snowstorm, electrical storm, earthquake, fire, flood, or hurricane. Design an evacuation plan in case one of these disasters strikes your home or community. Practice this plan until you can follow it properly.

9 Find out about the kinds of careers that require the use of first aid. Choose the career that interests you and learn about its purposes and responsibilities.

My signature

Leader's signature   Date badge completed

Group Sports

Complete six activities, including the two starred.

*1 Choose a group sport, such as basketball, field hockey, soccer, softball, or volleyball.
- ☐ Learn the rules of the game.
- ☐ Practice the skills and strategies needed to participate in your sport.

2 Visit a sports equipment store or look in a sports catalog and learn about the different types of equipment used and clothing worn in your sport.
- ☐ Find out what to look for in buying these items.
- ☐ Show that you know how to dress for this sport in warm, cool, hot, cold. windy, and rainy weather.

3 Trace the history and development of your sport. Find out what makes this sport special, the countries in which it is popular, the past and present star athletes, and the outstanding teams.

4 Learn the various team positions, where they play and what they do. Design a chart of the athletic field used to play this sport and indicate the position of each player.

5 Observe in person or on television two events involving this sport.
- ☐ Note three of the following: how the game is played, how it is scored, the number and position of players, how the team works together, the uniforms worn, or the equipment used.
- ☐ Record your feelings about this event and the new things you discovered.

*6 Demonstrate your ability to do the following:
- ☐ Select a safe place to play.
- ☐ Choose the proper warm-up exercises.
- ☐ Give first aid to an injured player.

7 With a group, plan a way to participate in this sport for fun and enjoyment, but give it your best. You might plan a game, tournament, or sports day.
☐ Make the game fair and safe.
☐ Show how well you can play together as a group.
☐ Discover ways that you can improve your play.

8 Discover what it is like to be a member of a team.
☐ Collect information (from books, magazine articles, newspaper clippings, athletes, coaches, etc.) on the type of diet, exercise, and training, and the give-and-take required for an athlete in this sport to meet the group's goals.
☐ Learn about the types of tournaments and competitions open to team members.

9 Learn how to keep score for or officiate at a sports event.
☐ Find out the duties of a scorekeeper or official and the training needed to do this job.
☐ Volunteer as a scorekeeper or official for a local sports event.

10 Write your own activity here, if you wish.

My signature

Leader's signature   Date badge completed

Healthy Eating

Complete six activities, including the three starred.

*1 Keep a diary of the foods you eat for at least three days. Include any snacks you have. Find out what the four food groups are and check to see if you had enough servings from each group.

OR Make a picture or word collage which tells about the foods you like to eat. Talk about your collage with others in your troop who do this activity. Check your foods with the four food groups. Which of your food habits need improving? Which are good habits?

2 Spend at least two lunch periods in the school cafeteria or lunchroom. Watch how much food is thrown away. Ask students why they throw away food. Meet with the cafeteria manager, parents, your teacher, or your leader and plan ways in which waste could be reduced. Carry out one of your plans.

*3 Make up a game to help younger children learn about the four food groups. Play the game with children.

OR Set up a display, make a mobile, or create a bulletin board promoting good eating habits for your school. Seek permission and share your plans ahead of time with the lunchroom staff, teachers, and/or principal so they can help.

*4 Have a tasting party in your troop. Select two or three foods from each of the four food groups. Pick unusual foods so everyone gets to taste something they have never eaten before.

OR Over a period of time, try six food items (fruits, vegetables, or main dishes) that are new to you. Keep a record of the texture, taste, look, and smell of each one. Choose your favorite. Bring it to a troop meeting to share with others.

5 Watch several hours of children's television programming. (Saturday mornings are a good time.) Count the number of food commercials that are shown. In what way do commercials teach good or poor eating habits? Decide which products advertised are nutritious and which are not. Don't just listen to what the commercials say: find the products and read the labels. Discuss the ingredients with others.

6 Make a holiday or party favor for a younger brother, sister, or Girl Scout. Fill your treat with nutritious, imaginative foods and nonfood items.

OR Plan, prepare, and serve a nutritious snack for a group of children or adults. Give out the recipe or serving suggestions.

7 Take a survey of the food products your family buys. Make a list of at least 20 of the foods. Find out who bought each one and what made the person choose it.

8 Collect pictures of different foods enjoyed in several areas of the world or parts of one country. Try at least one food or recipe from another area of the world or culture.

My signature

Leader's signature   Date badge completed

Hobbies and Pets

Many people have things they do just for fun. Often these activities have little or nothing to do with school or a job. Sometimes what was a leisure-time activity when someone was a child becomes a career in later years. In any case, a hobby starts as something you enjoy doing. If you enjoy collecting miniature cars, growing plants, or taking care of pets, you may earn any of the four badges described in this section.

Before starting, think about a hobby you already have, or one that you would like to have, or whether you would like to spend your time on learning how to take care of a pet. Think through the costs, the time involved, and the space needed, and then decide which of the following you wish to choose first:

- ☐ Pet care
- ☐ "Making" hobbies
- ☐ "Collecting" hobbies
- ☐ "Doing" hobbies

Pet Care

Complete six activities, including the one starred.

1   Because being a pet owner means taking responsibility for a pet as long as it lives, it is important to choose pets wisely. Identify six animals that would make good pets. Find out their life expectancy. Make a chart or poster showing a picture of each and describe what would make the ideal home for that animal.

Why would these six animals not make good pets: wolf, deer, raccoon, monkey, baby alligator, skunk?

*2   Take responsibility for a pet (your own or someone else's) by providing it with the right care — shelter, food, exercise, and grooming (if needed). Keep a record, for two months, of how you cared for this pet. Add to your list the kinds of things that must be done daily, monthly, and yearly, and why. Include in your record the cost of care and how you give the pet the love and attention it needs.

3   Find out about the kinds of accidents and illnesses most common to your pet and how to protect against them. Learn the signs of illness and how to contact a veterinarian. Learn how to administer medicine or give treatment to your pet.

OR Tell how to approach an animal if it is injured. Show how to restrain it when giving treatment without risk to you or the animal. Learn how to give first aid for the injuries most common to a pet.

4 Find out how many babies your pet might have, and how often. Find out the same information about another kind of animal. Compare the answers. In each case, how many young would be produced in nine years? Would you be able to find homes for that many animals? Find out what you should do if you don't want your pet to have babies.

5 Find out about the laws in your community that help pets, such as license and leash laws and laws against cruelty to animals, selling baby chicks and painted turtles, and keeping certain animals as pets. List other ways you think your community could help pets.

OR Pretend your pet is lost. Write a newspaper advertisement or notice to post, telling what your pet looks like, where it was lost, and how you can be reached. (For ideas, look at the "lost pet" notices in newspapers.)

6 Find out how many people in your community have careers dealing with pets. Visit one of these people on the job or invite her/him to tell you about the work she/he does.

OR Visit an animal shelter, veterinary hospital, or humane society and find out how these places help pets and humans too. Find out if there is something your troop can do to assist and do it.

7 Do something extra concerning your pet: Read stories or books about your pet, write a story about it, make a pet puppet and tell a story with it, or participate in a pet show.

OR Start a scrapbook of animals. Collect pictures of animals, articles or funny stories about animals, animal laws, animal problems, advertisements for animal movies, etc.

8 What is a good diet for your pet? Collect advertisements for pet food. What information do they give you about the nutritional needs of an animal? Read labels on pet food containers to find ingredients and compare them for food values. How do your pet's needs differ from others? How will these nutritional needs change as it grows older?

9 How do you "talk" to your pet? How do you show a pet what you want it to do? What signs does your pet use to tell you what it wants? Describe a situation in which you and your pet communicate with each other.

My signature

Leaders's signature   Date badge completed

"Making" Hobbies

(Examples. any of the arts — woodworking, sculpture, knitting, sketching, photography, weaving)

Complete activity one, then do all the others.

1 Since starting a hobby is different than doing an activity once or twice, ask yourself these questions first. Write down the answers and discuss them with your family or other adult.
   ☐ Is this hobby for fun?
   ☐ Can I afford it?
   ☐ Do I have space for it?
   ☐ Do I have a special talent I can develop?
   ☐ Do I have time for it?
   ☐ Are there any health and safety factors?

2 Choose the subject you are going to work in and make enough examples so that you can explain, write up, or demonstrate how to make the item. Share this with your troop or other group.

3 Find out about other people who work with the subject you choose, for example, other carpenters, other potters, etc. Attend an exhibit, read a book, or interview people involved.

4 Find out something about the history and development of your subject. Share this with others in some creative way.

5 Display, use, or organize your finished products in some way and write a short essay about how you enjoy the work you have made.

6 Find out the career possibilities that can come from making the item you chose. Interview someone or collect several clippings, stories, or pictures of people in a career related to your hobby. Do you think that you would like to turn your hobby into a career or keep it as a hobby?

My signature

Leaders's signature   Date badge completed

"Collecting" Hobbies

(Examples: rocks, shells, coins, stamps, autographs, postcards)

Complete activity one, then do all the others.

1   "Collecting" hobbies are one of the most popular. Ask yourself these questions first. Write down the answers and discuss them with your family or other adult.
   - ☐ Is the hobby fun?
   - ☐ Can I afford it?
   - ☐ Do I have the space for it?

2   Collect enough items so that you will learn something about the subject. Catalog your collection including the name or classification, when you acquired it, cost, if any, and something special about each item. Share the list with your troop.

3   Arrange, display, or mount your collection so that you are able to show it to others. If possible, display your collection for your troop or other group, or show it to someone in your home.

4   Find out something about other people who collect the same things you do. List the clubs, organizations, and/or magazines that refer to your kind of collection. If possible, meet and talk with other collectors, or exchange letters to discuss your collection.

5   Read books or magazines about your hobby to find out all you can about its history and development and other activities that can grow out of this hobby. Present this in some creative way to your troop or group.

6   Create your own activity about your special hobby.

My signature

Leaders's signature   Date badge completed

"Doing" Hobbies

(Examples: singing in a choir, games, swimming or other sports, playing a musical instrument, cooking, gardening, hiking, letter writing [pen pals], reading, bird-watching)

Complete activity one, then do all the others.

1   "Doing" hobbies need to have some questions answered too. Write down your answers to these questions and discuss with your family or other adult.

☐ Is it for fun?

☐ Can I afford it?

☐ Do I have space for it?

☐ Where do I do it?

☐ Can I do it alone? or with others?

☐ Do I have time for it?

☐ Are there safety factors to consider?

2   Select your hobby and do it often enough or for a long enough period of time so that you can explain, write up, or demonstrate how it is done. Share this with your troop or other group in some manner.

3   Learn something about the history and development of your hobby, and about some people who have had it as a hobby.

4   Find out about the possible careers related to your hobby. If possible, interview someone or collect pictures and stories about people in careers similar to your hobby.

5   Participate in something with other people who also share your hobby, for example, sing with a choral music group, hike with others, join a photography show or exhibit, go to a garden or flower exhibit, etc.

6   Create your own activity specifically related to your hobby.

My signature

Leader's signature   Date badge completed

Home Living

Complete six activities.

1 Make something to show a family's life story.
   - ☐ Label important events in the family (birth of children, a move, starting school, marriage, divorce, graduations).
   - ☐ Select two of the events and discuss with others the changes they made in the family.

2 Watch several television programs or movies about families.
   - ☐ Look for the jobs each family member does, the way decisions are made, discussions between adults and children, the ways families share and help each member, and how they solve problems.
   - ☐ Talk about how the families were like or unlike families you know.

3 Switch home tasks with an adult at home.
   - ☐ Take care of several home tasks usually done by an adult for at least one week.
   - ☐ Invite an adult to take part in something you do, such as a troop meeting or after-school activity.
   - ☐ Talk together about what each of you learned, what surprised you, what you enjoyed or disliked.

OR Get to know an older person well. (This could be a grandparent, older friend, or adopted grandparent in a senior citizens' home.) Plan and do an activity together that both of you enjoy.

4 Collect or tape-record definitions of a homemaker. Do this with several people including some women and men and some girls and boys your own age. Discuss your own definition.

5 Do something extra special on several occasions for each person in your family without their knowing about it. Share what you did with your leader or troop and tell what the reaction of each person was (if you know it).

OR Make a traditional holiday craft object from your own family's heritage. Plan a way to tell others about this item.

6 Find out about several agencies that help families in the community. Find out about the people who work in these agencies, the kinds of help they give to families, the training and education they need, and their salary ranges. Add the information you find to a troop career file.

7 Take a look at household tasks with family members. Talk about each person's responsibilities and activities outside the home (jobs, school, hobbies, volunteer work, etc.). Then list the tasks done at home and plan ways to cooperate and share to get the work done. Follow your plan for several weeks, revising it if necessary.

8 Make up a skit, short story, or picture story about family life 15 years from now. Include people you would like to be there and what each person might be doing.

9 Collect pictures and/or stories from newspapers and magazines that show how families spend their time and money. Include pictures of families from your own city or town and state and from different parts of the United States and the world.

☐ Discuss which customs are like or unlike your family's.

☐ Why do you think this is so?

☐ Share your findings with others.

My signature

Leader's signature   Date badge completed

Household Whiz

Complete six activities, including the three starred.

1 Interview the oldest member of your family or community about their growing up years. Find out what household laborsaving techniques and products have been invented since then. Find out how the changes in housekeeping have changed family life. Share your discoveries with others.

*2 For at least two weeks, in addition to your regular chores, do one of the following household tasks in your home or the home of someone you know who could use your help: shopping, meal preparation, laundry, gardening, light cleaning. Ask family members to help you evaluate how well you took care of your tasks.

*3 Conduct a safety check of your home. Spot and correct hazards with the help of family members. Be alert for problem areas that might endanger a family member who has a disability or who is ill, an infant or toddler, or an elderly person who has problems with eyesight or walking. List the following information and post it in a handy spot: phone numbers of police, fire department, poison control center, doctor, ambulance.

4 For a month, keep a written record of the money you receive, spend, and save. Decide whether or not you need to change your spending habits. If you do, decide on a plan. Ask an adult what financial records need to be kept for a household to run smoothly.

5 If you don't already do it, take care of washing your own clothes or those of the family several times. Follow the directions on the labels of the laundry products you use. Replace a button and repair a seam or tear.

*6 Discuss with your family the six largest household purchases it has made. Do a bit of detective work for one item as if you had to replace it. Decide exactly what you want. Find out where you can get the best price. Plan how to pay for your purchase. Decide how you would complain about your purchase if it did not work properly.

OR Choose a vegetable or fruit that is sold in fresh, frozen, and canned form. Note and compare the unit price for each. Decide which is the most economical. Prepare and taste all three forms and decide which you like best and why.

7 Find out about services available to consumers in your community at low cost. Make a listing of all the places you discover with information about these services. Give your list to people in your community who could use it.

8 Discuss and make something that shows the kinds of decisions families make. Include the people involved in making decisions or solving problems and the way the decision or problem was worked out.

OR Interview a few mothers who work outside the home and a few who are full-time homemakers. Find out how the household tasks, such as laundry, shopping, cleaning, repairs, gardening, meal preparation, and bill paying are arranged in each family. How are tasks shared with other family members?

9 Explore the ways energy is used in your home. Observe and record how family members use gas, oil, water, paper products, electricity, or other natural resources. Do an energy-saving project for your home, troop, school class, or community.

10 Make, repair, repaint, or refinish an object to beautify your home. Use a method you've never tried before. Compare the cost of doing it yourself, having it done by someone else, or buying the object.

My signature

Leader's signature   Date badge completed

Individual Sports

Complete six activities, including the two starred.

*1 Choose an individual sport, such as bowling, cycling, frisbee, gymnastics, ice or roller skating, swimming, tennis, track and field, or tumbling.
- ☐ Learn the rules and be able to explain them to others.
- ☐ Practice the skills until you feel comfortable doing them.

*2 Show how to select, use, care for, and store the equipment and clothing needed to participate in your sport.
- ☐ Visit a sports equipment store or look in a sports catalog to learn more about these items.
- ☐ Find out the facilities that are available for your use.

3 Read about the history of your sport. Discover in which countries this sport is popular and its famous past and present athletes.

OR Find out as much as you can about your favorite sports hero and write a short story about her/him.

4 Learn and practice several warm-up exercises used to loosen the muscles of your body.
- ☐ Tell the purpose of each exercise.
- ☐ Show others how these exercises are done.

5 Attend or watch on television two events featuring this sport.
- ☐ Note three of the following: how the event is played, how it is scored, the number of players, the types of uniforms worn, the equipment or playing area used.
- ☐ Write or make something that describes your feelings about one of these events.

6 Find out what injuries occur most often from participating in this sport.
- ☐ Show first aid for at least two of these injuries.
- ☐ Discuss the safety tips you would give to help prevent them.

7 Participate in this sport with others by taking part in a tournament, club, play day, intramural program, or team.
   ☐ Follow the rules of safety and fair play.
   ☐ Demonstrate your ability to cooperate with others.
   ☐ Find out how climate affects your ability to play.

8 Learn to play and teach two games that are similar to your sport. You might want to select a game that is played in another country.

9 Find out what the life of an athlete is really like.
   ☐ Search sources for information on the diet, exercise, and training needed for an athlete in this sport.
   ☐ Learn about the types of tournaments and amateur and professional opportunities available for athletes in this sport.

10 Write your own activity here, if you wish.

My signature

Leader's signature   Date badge completed

Personal Health

Complete six activities, including the two starred.

*1 Select a nutrient, such as protein, carbohydrate, fat, vitamin, or mineral.
- ☐ Discover why it is important to the body.
- ☐ Locate and list foods that contain this nutrient. Star the foods that contain no artificial ingredients and those that contain no sugar.
- ☐ Make a habit of including these foods in your diet.

OR Prepare a meatless meal for a family.
- ☐ Be sure to include the needed nutrients listed above and use the four food groups as a guide.
- ☐ What benefits does this type of meal have on your health and your food bill?

*2 Learn how to take your temperature, pulse, blood pressure, and respiration (breathing rate).
- ☐ Find out what is normal for you.
- ☐ Teach one of these skills to another person.

3 Keep a personal feelings journal for at least three weeks.
- ☐ Record your thoughts about things you do and how you get along with other people.
- ☐ Write down things that make you happy, calm, proud, sad, angry, jealous, etc.
- ☐ Look over your journal after three weeks and see if it tells you something you didn't know about yourself.

4 Compile a personal health record. Include immunizations, allergies, history of diseases and accidents, family health history, and hospital stays. Keep your health record in a safe and handy place. Keep it up-to-date.

5 Plan a skit, puppet show, or display that tells others about the importance of good dental health care. Your presentation may include: brushing and flossing teeth, eating nutritious foods, visiting the dentist, etc. Present this information in an interesting way.

6 Set up a personal care schedule and use it. Include combing, brushing, and shampooing hair; bathing; brushing teeth; cleaning nails and feet; having health examinations, etc.

7 Demonstrate good posture while walking, standing, sitting, and lifting. You might use a full-length mirror to tell if your posture is good. Learn why good posture is important, and how it relates to good health, good appearance, and feeling good about yourself.

8 Discover how you have grown over the years.
- ☐ Collect old and recent photographs of yourself or talk to an older family member or relative.
- ☐ Note your growth in height, weight, appearance, etc.
- ☐ Learn what physical and emotional changes will take place as you become a teenager.
- ☐ What did you discover about yourself and what changes do you think you'll observe in the future?

OR Survey at least five people.
- ☐ Find out how they feel about teenagers.
- ☐ Make note of the most common positive and the most common problem feelings.
- ☐ How do these feelings compare with yours?

9 Find out why people smoke or use drugs or alcohol. Learn how this can affect their health. Share what you have discovered with others.

10 Design your own fitness program for a week. Include one or more of the following:
- ☐ exercises, such as sit-ups or jumping jacks
- ☐ rhythmic activities, such as dancing or rope jumping
- ☐ active games, such as tag or relays
- ☐ sports activities, such as swimming or jogging

Learn the purpose of each exercise and/or activity and how it contributes to fitness and good health. Plan how to make fitness a lifetime activity.

My signature

Leader's signature   Date badge completed

Sports Sampler

Complete six activities, including the two starred.

1 Discover which sports are available for you and others in your community.
- ☐ Search for sports that you can participate in alone and those that involve a team or a group.
- ☐ Find a way to tell others about the sports: what skills are necessary to participate alone and how a team works.

2 Read one of the following books and be able to tell others what it was about:
- ☐ a sports story or collection of stories
- ☐ a biography of an athlete or coach
- ☐ the history of a sport or the Olympic Games

3 Find out the proper attire and/or equipment needed to participate in four different sports activities.
- ☐ Compare attire for warm, cool, hot, or cold weather.
- ☐ Pick equipment that protects different parts of the body. Tell what it does and why it is needed.

*4 Discuss the rules of fair play and safety when taking part in or watching sports.
- ☐ Keep a list of these rules.
- ☐ Decide what action should be taken if the rules are broken.
- ☐ Set a fair and safe example for others.

5 Show that you are prepared to help an injured person. Be able to treat three of the following injuries:
- ☐ cut lip or skinned knee
- ☐ nosebleed
- ☐ broken tooth
- ☐ blister
- ☐ sprained ankle
- ☐ loss of consciousness

*6 Demonstrate your ability to do at least three of the following sports skills:
- ☐ running at least 55 meters—or about 60 yards
- ☐ dribbling a basketball with right or left hand or alternating hands
- ☐ balancing on one leg, on the balance beam, on a bicycle, or with a book on your head
- ☐ jumping as high and as far as you can
- ☐ throwing as far as you can, at a target
- ☐ catching a low ball and/or a flyball
- ☐ kicking a stationary ball and/or a moving ball
- ☐ volleying against a backboard, in tennis, or in table tennis

Practice at least one skill you cannot do very well at present.

7 Take a survey of at least ten people.
- ☐ Ask them what kind of exercise or sport they participate in and why they do it.

OR Be able to explain why exercise and sports participation are important to good health.

8 Attend a sports event, such as a basketball or baseball game, swimming meet, tennis match, or figure skating show.

OR Watch one of these events on television.

9 Help plan a fun-filled play day, games festival, or tournament. Include activities for all ages. Participate in a variety of the activities or be a games leader or referee.

10 Create a sports career word hunt.
- ☐ Find out the careers available in the sports field.
- ☐ Make a word hunt or word search puzzle using these careers.
- ☐ Get others to complete your puzzle.

OR Talk to a sports person, such as an athlete, coach, athletic trainer, official, sportswriter, scorekeeper, or equipment manager. Find out about her/his work and the training needed for that job.

My signature

Leader's signature   Date badge completed

Tending Toddlers

Complete six activities, including the two starred.

1   Invite a group of parents to discuss their thoughts or feelings about being parents, the first time they held their babies, what makes an infant feel secure, the importance of talking and playing with a child, how a child changed their lives, and any other topic you would like to discuss.

*2   Spend time with a young child or infant on several occasions. Watch the child carefully. Keep a discovery diary and record:

What I discovered _____ can do alone:

(name of child)

_____

_____

What I discovered _____ can do with help:

(name of child)

_____

_____

What I discovered _____ can't do for

(name of child)

herself/himself: _____

_____

I was surprised to see _____ do _____

(name of child)   (what)

_____

Feelings _____ expressed were:
(name of child)

_____

_____

I never knew that _____

_____

I enjoyed _____

_____

Things that I did to make _____ happy were:
(name of child)

_____

_____

3 Make a "This Is My Life" book or scrapbook of your favorite activities and experiences at different ages.

*4 Demonstrate that you know how to hold, feed, and dress an infant. Do each of these things for a baby several times.

5 Talk to a school nurse or other health care worker about the immunizations children get and why. Find out what health records are necessary for children. Check to see that you have all the immunizations required. Make your own record, if one is not available, filling in all the information your family can help you with.

6 In small groups, talk about and list all the things both women and men can do for children. Collect and mount pictures that show both women and men doing many types of activities with children. Donate your pictures to a place where they could be used.

7 Decide what supplies you would need if you were taking an infant or toddler on a picnic or other all-day outing. Explain why you would include each item.

8 Prepare and serve several healthy meals or snacks to an infant, toddler, or small child.

9 Find out what household items can be dangerous for an infant or toddler. Make a list of these items and then find out how they are stored in your home. If possible, do a safety check in a home where there is an infant or toddler.

OR Go through a toy store or catalog and check for toys that would be safe and those which would be dangerous for children under three years old. Decide on a way to share your findings with adults.

My signature

Leader's signature   Date badge completed

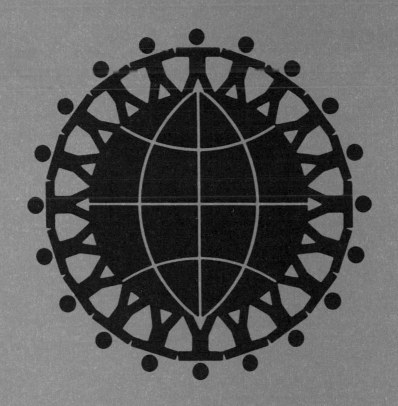

The World of
People

Dabbler

Complete one activity in each group.

A.1 Show where your family or a family you know has lived at least as far back as the grandparents. Add the dates if you can.

2 Choose one person from the past and imagine being that person for a day. Find a way to show what you might wear and do.

B.1 Pretend your community needs someone to be a dogcatcher of children's little dogs, a tricycle traffic police person, and a sandbox watcher. Choose one of these jobs. Make up some rules related to your job that you feel young children should obey. Beside each rule, write what should be done if someone breaks it.

2 Why do so many national flags have little moons on them? Why are so many red, white, and blue? Make or draw flags from two countries and explain the meanings of the colors, shapes, and pictures on them. Or design your own flag and explain the meaning behind your choice of color and design.

C.1 Make or draw a hat, badge, uniform, or tool for two or more workers who help people in your community. Use what you have made to tell younger children how these people help them, their families, their schools, and/or older people.

2 Talk to someone who works for your community to find out about her/his job. Ask about similar paid jobs and ways to volunteer to help with this work.

D.1 Make ten or more word cards for a language you do not know. On one side of the card, write a word and how to say it. On the other side, place a drawing of the word. Using the word cards, teach yourself or someone else the new words.

2 Attend a festival or event held by an ethnic group in your community or watch one on television. You might see a Pueblo Green Corn dance, a Chinese New Year's parade, a Scottish Highlands' game, or a Kwanza celebration. Afterwards, design a poster for next year's event to show some of the things people could expect to see.

E.1 Visit a grocery or supermarket, taking pencil and paper with you. Check labels of cans and boxes. Make a list of the countries these products come from and compare it with similar lists made by other girls in your troop.

2 Design a set of color postcards or drawings to show trees, flowers, animals, houses, or important buildings in one country. Ask someone to guess the country or area of the world.

F.1 In the World Association there are over 100 countries and more than 60 of them start with one of these letters: B, C, G, I, L, M, P, S, or U. On a globe or a world map, locate at least 15 countries that begin with these letters.

2 Prepare a booklet to introduce Girl Scouting to a friend. Include some information she might need or want to know. Add a description of an occasion or activity you have especially enjoyed in Girl Scouting.

G.1 Where would you like to go? Make up a poem, song, or picture that shows what you might take, see, and do on a vacation trip to a place of your own choosing.

2 Take three different short walks. On each walk, go in a different direction and find at least two things you have never noticed there before.

My signature

Leader's signature   Date badge completed

Active Citizen

Complete four activities.

1 Prepare a display of citizenship symbols. Choose two nations and include pictures or drawings that have special meaning to each country and that show the diversity of people there. Try to choose countries located in different parts of the globe.

2 Talk to someone in your family or community who chose to leave her/his country or home to be free; or read a book or see a movie or television program about a flight to freedom. Share what you have learned through an original artwork of any kind.

3 Explore patriotic holidays around the world. Find out how patriotic holidays are observed in various parts of the United States and in other nations. Share with your troop information about two or more of these holidays or hold a patriotic celebration special to one of these places.

4 Choose an issue that is important in your community, such as pollution; or the condition of roads, new or old buildings, or playgrounds, etc. Collect and read some newspaper articles and photo stories about the issue. Listen to someone talk about the issue on radio, television, or in a public place. Or you may talk to a friend or neighbor who knows something about it. If there is more than one side, be sure to find out about a different point of view. Make something to show how people in your community feel about the issue. Decide how you feel about the issue and be able to explain why you feel this way.

5 Find out how to do three or more of these:
   - ☐ report a stray animal
   - ☐ report a crime
   - ☐ obtain a pet license
   - ☐ register a bicycle
   - ☐ locate the owner of a vacant lot or nearby woods
   - ☐ get free dental care

6 For three days, keep a record of all the laws you must follow — for traffic, in schools or parks, even in your own home. Consider changing at least one of these laws so that more people would benefit. Write up your new law and be able to explain why your law is better than the present one.

OR Attend a courtroom trial. Find out about the rights and responsibilities of the judge, jury, defendant, and prosecutor.

OR Invite a lawyer, judge, probation or parole officer, or member of the Legal Aid Society to come to your troop meeting or visit this person at her/his office. Ask about her/his work, the legal services offered, and the way these services help people. Inquire about your legal rights and be prepared to explain them to someone.

7 Add your activity here, if you wish.

My signature

Leader's signature   Date badge completed

Around the Town

Complete six activities.

1 Prepare an advertisement for newspapers, magazines, radio, or television to attract someone your age to move to your community. Include things you enjoy seeing and doing that another girl might like, too.

2 Investigate the route of two or more of the following: transportation systems (trains, buses, ferries); delivery vans or trucks; collection services (for garbage, leaves, paper, etc.).

☐ For a transportation system, find out the route and the stops closest to your home.

☐ For a delivery or collection service, find out what days and times the van or truck comes by your home and the route it follows on those days.

3 Find a way to show others the rich variety among people in your community and/or the surrounding area. The variety may be illustrated by family and street names, languages spoken, etc.

4 Find out about the local/regional food heritage. Locate recipes or cookbooks from your public library, historical society, restaurants, delicatessens, women's groups, newspapers, or longtime residents. Draw up menus for two meals, write down three traditional recipes, or prepare one dish.

5 Make a community service survey. Keep track for a week of all the services your community provides that you use.

OR Make a map of your local area indicating on it all the community services found there.

6 Visit a center that provides free or inexpensive resources and/or services to your community. Afterwards, prepare some written or illustrated information to promote these services within the community.

7 What plans are being made for future changes in your community: new buildings, schools, playgrounds, or roads?

☐ Ask a representative of your local government, newspaper, or citizens' group what changes are being proposed.

☐ Talk to someone else you know to find out how they feel about the possible changes.

☐ Decide how you feel about some of your community's plans for the future. Be able to explain the reasons for your opinions.

8 Imagine you are the mayor or other town/city official and prepare a list of several things you want to see changed and improved in your community.

9 By yourself or with friends within or outside your troop, figure out something to do for your neighborhood or community, its people, buildings, or grounds. Spend at least two hours on completing your neighborhood action project.

My signature

Leader's signature   Date badge completed

Girl Scouting Everywhere

Complete six activities.

1 Ask your leader, another volunteer, or a staff member of your Girl Scout council to take you on an imaginary or actual trip around your council to visit important council locations and to meet people who work with Girl Scouts. Find out how many Girl Scout councils there are in the United States and which ones touch the borders of your council.

2 Talk to council or national volunteers to find out about their volunteer work in Girl Scouting and why they are doing it.

3 Put on some skits, prepare a booklet, or make a mural illustrating some of the experiences of Juliette Low and/or the Baden-Powells.

4 Show you know some of the symbols, ceremonies, and/or ways that are special to Girl Scouts in this country and, if possible, Girl Scouts and Girl Guides in many parts of the world.

5 Look in your handbook to find out about Thinking Day. Participate in planning and carrying out an activity or special event for Thinking Day.

6 See an audiovisual that shows the Girl Scout national centers or World Association centers or talk to someone who has visited one of these centers. Tell what you would like to do if you could visit one of these centers.

7 Learn the Girl Guide or Girl Scout Promise in one other language and in its English translation.

8 Find out about Girl Guide and Girl Scout pins and uniforms around the world. First, be able to explain the meaning of each part of the World Association pin that Girl Guides/Girl Scouts everywhere wear. Then, look for pictures of Girl Guide/Girl Scout pins and uniforms in your handbook, **Trefoil Round the World,** and **The Wide World of Girl Guiding and Girl Scouting** and make comparisons with your own pin and uniform.

9 Make up a game to help Brownies learn where Girl Guides/Girl Scouts live. Use your game at a neighborhood event, as a wide game at day camp, or in helping Brownies bridge to Juniors.

My signature

Leader's signature   Date badge completed

Hands Around the World

Complete four activities.

1 Make a chart, diagram, or list showing five different volunteer and/or staff jobs in Girl Scouting. Be able to tell two things each person does on the job. Decide which job you would like to have and explain what you would do for Girl Scouting in that job.

2 Participate in a local, council, or intercouncil Girl Scout event in a special way. Help in the planning and organizing of the event, and share your experiences with others.

OR Set up and participate in a troop greeting committee to invite and welcome new members. Have special activities or events to include new girls in your troop. Be a buddy for a girl new to your troop for at least one month.

3 Design a series of posters, cards, or pictures for younger girls, illustrating and explaining important people, places, and events in Girl Scouting in your council, on a national level, and/or throughout the world.

4 Talk to an adult Girl Scout or visit your council office. Find out what adult Girl Scouts do and have done in Girl Scouting. Ask about the services of your council, national headquarters, National Board of Directors, the National Council, World Association of Girl Guides and Girl Scouts, and national and world centers. Share the information with your troop.

OR Make a map of your council. Show the cities and towns within it, the council office and/or program centers, and places important to Girl Scouting. Be sure to indicate the councils that border on your council. Try to show as many important geographic features, such as rivers, as possible.

OR Become an expert on Girl Guiding/Girl Scouting in another country. Know about how Girl Guiding/Girl Scouting started in the country, age groupings, Promise and motto, uniforms, and favorite activities. Learn a game, song, craft, recipe, or activity that girls in the country like and find a way to share it with your troop or other Girl Scouts. You may use **Trefoil Round the World** and **The Wide World of Girl Guiding and Girl Scouting** to help you.

5 Build a model or prepare a diorama of one of the World Association centers or Juliette Low's birthplace. You may want to add landscaping to indicate the surroundings or take off the roof to get an interior view. Your model does not need to be made to scale, but the center you choose should be easily recognized. Display your center or use it to explain to Brownie Girl Scouts what you know about the center you have portrayed.

6 Add your own activity here, if you wish.

My signature

Leader's signature   Date badge completed

Junior Citizen

Complete six activities.

1 Assist someone in her/his efforts to become a citizen. Try to attend the official ceremony with this person and celebrate with her/him afterwards.

OR Find out what someone must do to become a citizen. Think of ways you could be of help to people becoming citizens.

2 Talk with someone who has been a citizen in a country outside the United States. Find out what it is like to be a citizen in another country.

3 Discover something about your flag: ways to fold, hold, or carry it, or meanings and information about flags of the United States, now and in the past. Hold a flag ceremony or Court of Awards that will demonstrate what you and other girls in your troop know about flags.

4 Have a campaign for a real or imaginary candidate. You might make a poster or give a speech to tell about yourself or someone else. Try to persuade as many girls in your troop as possible that your candidate is best. When several girls have had a chance to campaign for their candidates, take a vote for the most popular one.

5 Talk to someone who is helping run an election campaign, is on the local board of elections, or is an active member of a political party or the League of Women Voters. Find out about this person's work and why she/he is doing it.

6 Visit a police station or talk with a police officer to find out how the law operates in your community. Ask about laws that affect children.

7 Design rules, regulations, or laws that might be needed for two of these situations:
   - ☐ a bicycle path near a truck highway
   - ☐ a strawberry farm next to a school
   - ☐ a zoo with no cages or fences
   - ☐ a town where everyone owns airplanes and no one has a car
   - ☐ a five-story apartment building with no elevators and only one inside and one outside stairway
   - ☐ pets in the first moon town

8 Write to or visit a government office near your home or far away. Ask about the services it provides, free information it offers, and kinds of work done in that office.

9 Design and carry out a small project to show you care about your neighborhood and the people who live there. You may do your project on your own or with the help of others. Spend at least two hours carrying out your project.

My signature

Leader's signature   Date badge completed

Local Lore

Complete four activities.

1 Design a family album. Include a family tree. For each person on the family tree, use the full name, including maiden name for women, and each person's birth, marriage, and death dates and places. Try to go back more than two generations. Include photos and mementos and write down any interesting stories you learn, jobs people held, etc.

2 Do one or more of the following projects.
   ☐ Pick one important event that affected your family, either in the past or present. Describe this event in a special way. Share it with your patrol or troop.
   ☐ Begin a "wisdom list" of quotations, sayings, and advice your parents, grandparents, and other older people have told you, or prepare a booklet containing funny stories and amusing sayings they have shared with you.
   ☐ Start a diary of your own memories. Write about some important events from your childhood and recent happenings. Write these events as stories you think will be of interest to a girl 50 years from now to help her understand about life today. Include photos or other mementos.

3 Do one or more of the following projects.
   ☐ Dip or mold candles or make soap. Find out about the sources of waxes and scents used, if possible.
   ☐ Try one type of needlework, such as embroidery, needlepoint, quilting, tatting, etc.
   ☐ Sing and/or play three songs from former times or places. Find out about folk instruments, such as the recorder, thumb piano, koto, and dulcimer, which were used in the past and may still be played today.
   ☐ Braid or hook a rug or wall hanging.
   ☐ Plant an herb or kitchen garden.

4 Preserve one or more buildings with pictures or photographs. Mount a display of your pictures or photographs.

OR Plan and guide a walking tour to include these buildings.

5 Locate an early map of your town or area and compare it with a present-day map. Look for areas that have remained the same and those that have changed. Construct something that shows the changes in your community.

6 Visit an old graveyard. Begin a list of unusual first and/or last names found on the early tombstones. Prepare a chart of names with birth and death dates for at least two families buried in the graveyard you have visited. Write down any ideas about historical events or the lives of the people that you can discover from the information on the tombstones.

OR Visit a local historical society site, museum, home, or ship. When you become familiar enough with it, give a tour through it to a small group of friends or strangers.

7 Add your own activity here, if you wish.

My signature

Leader's signature   Date badge completed

My Community

Complete four activities.

1 Plan a walking tour or bike tour of your area. Figure out the interesting, beautiful, and/or unusual things to see along the way.

   Design a pamphlet to describe the tour and include a map and/or careful directions and illustrations or photos, or you can lead a group on your tour.

2 Explore the richness of the many peoples of your community or county by visiting the library, historical society, town or city hall, places of worship, museums, state or country fairs, restaurants, delicatessens, bakeries, and/or specialty stores. Find out about the unique contributions made to your community by individuals and/or groups of people. Share what you have learned with your troop.

3 Look carefully at the pedestrian and vehicle traffic flow at two or more points in your community. Choose one point in your community where you think you might change and improve the traffic flow. Design a diagram or model to show your ideas.

4 What does your community produce or provide that other parts of the country would miss if your community disappeared overnight? What do other communities or other parts of the world produce that you could not be without? Think of the many products or services originating in your community and those which must come from outside. Design a display, to tell about everyone's interdependence — what others depend on from your community and what you depend on from communities near and far.

5 Solve a community problem. You may use the situation below or develop one from your own community. Some people want to restore Main Street. Here are the characters and how they feel:

☐ mayor—wants the project because it would make more jobs
☐ police chief—against it because of increased traffic
☐ school principal—against it because of danger to children
☐ truck driver—for it because trucks cannot use Main Street now
☐ residents—some for the community improvement and some against increased pollution

Try to find a solution to the problem by having a discussion, debate, or open forum with the cast of characters.

6 Investigate a local transportation system (bus, train, ferry, etc.). Talk to someone who works on it. Find out what job the person does, and how the system is kept safe and efficient. Or talk to someone who uses this system to find out why she/he uses it, how she/he feels about the transportation, and suggestions she/he has for improving the system. Put together your findings to share through local media or with your troop.

7 Design one or more of these communities:

☐ a village high in the mountains where there are frequent avalanches
☐ a city in a desert far away from a large supply of water
☐ a farming area close to a forest filled with large and small wildlife
☐ a settlement on a river that often has high flooding
☐ a group of towns on a planet that moves noticeably closer to the sun each year

You can see that each of these communities has a serious problem. Whichever community you choose, work out a solution to its problem in the design you make.

8 Add your own activity here, if you wish.

My signature

Leader's signature   Date badge completed

My Heritage

Complete six activities.

1 Ask older people you know to tell stories of their lives, a day or a special event they would like to relive, or to remember stories they have heard told in the family.

OR Make a family picture collection of some of your ancestors and/or other relatives.

2 Find out the meanings of three or more names. Here are some names to try: first, middle, or family names; nicknames; names of streets, community areas, counties, states, or nations; or names of geographical features, such as mountains, glaciers, lakes, or rivers. _Completed_

3 Hunt, for at least an hour, in nearby places for signs of history. Poke in corners and underneath things, look high and low, to find out if someone was there before 1900. With pencil and/or camera, keep a record of your findings to share with your troop.

4 Ask people in your community to tell you stories of your community's past. Share these stories with others in an interesting way.

5 Make a toy, play a game, or learn a dance that one of your ancestors might have enjoyed.

6 Visit an antique collector or dealer. Decide what kind of antiques you like: furniture, kitchen utensils, toys, games, art objects, etc.

7 Explore your community's past by learning a legend, song, or craft which might have been used 100 or more years ago. Share it with your troop.

8 See if your community or a nearby area now has or once had one of these historic routes: pioneer trail, American Indian trail, underground railroad stop, cattle route, abandoned railroad bed, canal, or other historic trails or waterways.

   Visit the historic route or show where it would have been on a local map.

   Try to find some information about the use of the route to share with your troop.

9 Make several tombstone rubbings.

OR Collect photographs of unique tombstone markers.

OR Start a collection of unusual epitaphs.

My signature

Leader's signature   Date badge completed

On My Way

Complete six activities.

1 Choose a spot away from your hometown that you would like to visit for a weekend.
   ☐ Decide how you will get there, the people and places you want to visit, what you will wear and take with you.
   ☐ Then, if possible, go to the place you have chosen.

2 Choose three countries in different parts of the world you would like to visit.
   ☐ Find out for which countries you will need a passport and/or visa.
   ☐ Find out what immunizations you will need for each country you have chosen.

3 Pretend you are visiting a place you have never been before, either in or outside the United States.
   ☐ Write an imaginary letter from this place about the people you might meet and what you could do and see if you were traveling there.

OR ☐ Design two or more postcards from this place to send to a friend. Add messages to tell your friend about the postcard pictures.

4 Imagine your troop is traveling to a place whose language none of you can speak. No one there can speak your language, either.
   ☐ Make up a skit having some girls in it from your troop and some from the hostess country. In your skit show ways you would communicate with each other to find a hotel or campground, to order a meal, to see famous tourist sights, to catch a train, to play in a park, etc.

5 Choose three or more food specialties from various regions of the United States or countries around the world.
   ☐ Before trying one of these foods, imagine what it tastes like and try to describe it to someone.
   ☐ Prepare and/or taste one of these specialties or have a tasting party.

6 Imagine going on a week's vacation in at least three of the settings below. You may take only ten articles of clothing for each trip. Figure out what clothing you will take and compare your list with those of other girls in your troop.

- [ ] grandmother's farm in the summer
- [ ] a cabin in snowy mountains
- [ ] an alligator farm in a swamp area
- [ ] a wooded campground in fall
- [ ] a city hotel in winter
- [ ] a raft or a barge on a river
- [ ] a ranch in early spring

7 Plan your own vacation.

- [ ] Prepare a schedule for what you would do and the people you would see on a week's vacation to one or more places.
- [ ] Using a map, show someone how you will get there or figure out the round-trip distance(s) in kilometers.

8 Find out about travelers' or visitors' services in your community.

- [ ] Show someone around who is visiting your community or put together a packet about your community for a traveler.

9 Visit a travel agent or ask one to come to a troop meeting. Find out:

- [ ] how a travel agent helps plan trips
- [ ] what an itinerary looks like
- [ ] ideas for getting to meet residents of an area while traveling
- [ ] varieties of transportation used in traveling
- [ ] what training is needed for a travel agency job

My signature

Leader's signature   Date badge completed

Peoples of the United States

Complete six activities.

1 Make a map, chart, or poster that shows the places of origin of the people in your neighborhood or community.

OR Take a survey of at least ten people you know in your apartment house, block, neighborhood, school, or Girl Scout troop. Find out how many were born outside the United States, have (or had) parents or grandparents from another country, and/or speak more than one language. Keep track of the countries, languages, and racial groups represented in your survey.

2 Learn a little of a language new to you. You may have help from the Girl Scout **Say It in Another Language** cassette, from a friend, or from someone living or visiting in your community. Teach someone else at least five words in the new language you have learned.

3 By any means you know, except by speaking or writing, communicate at least three of the following to other members of your troop:
☐ How I get to school.
☐ Will you go with me to the grocery store?
☐ I want to find an after-school job.
☐ My grandmother lives in a nice house.
☐ My puppy has run away.

Think up and communicate two more things you might want to say if you could not speak the language most people around you spoke or were not able to talk.

4 Make a display to represent some parts of your own cultural heritage. Your display might include objects, photographs, drawings, or handicrafts.

OR Share your own cultural heritage by demonstrating a handicraft or a dance, or by playing music for others.

5 Look for ways in which one or more cultural groups express themselves through art. Do one of the following:

- [ ] Visit a local museum, art show, or musical or dance program.
- [ ] Visit a local craftsman, artist, musician, dancer, writer, or actor or
  invite her/him to your troop meeting. Talk to this artist about
  her/his work, interests, and successes.
- [ ] Listen to a living artist, musician, writer, or actor on records,
  tapes, radio, or television. See how she/he expresses the feeling
  of her/his people.
- [ ] Go to one or more stores and visit several departments, such as
  the art, record, book, furniture, china, and clothing departments.
  Note which items are representative of or come from various
  cultures in this country and countries around the world.

6 Design a colorful advertisement to invite visitors to a celebration or
festivities of your own ethnic group.

OR Make a model or mural illustrating a holiday celebration you have
seen or would like to visit.

7 With your troop, patrol, or small group, prepare a calendar for at least
three months of the year, showing the ethnic events and festivities in
your community.

8 Look through at least one publication, newspaper, magazine, pamphlet, or book put out by and/or for a specific ethnic, cultural, or
language group. If the publication is printed in a language you do not
know, try to find someone who can read it and give you a general idea
of the contents.

9 Using a diary or small notebook, jot down some of your feelings about
people whose cultural background is not the same as your own. Do
you find you can share and talk easily with friends whose backgrounds differ from yours? Are there some concerns or fears you
have about some peoples? What are your reactions when you watch
a television program that has people from various cultures? You will
want to look at your feelings honestly and try to figure out why you
react as you do. It is not necessary to share your diary with anyone.

My signature

Leader's signature   Date badge completed

The World in My Community

Complete four activities.

1 Design or use a prepared map of your neighborhood, block, county, parish, town, or a nearby community. Mark on your map evidences of the contributions of various ethnic groups, either in the present or the past: architecture, crops, businesses, stores, street names, trees and plants, statues, artworks, boats, etc.

2 How does your cultural background affect your life? Talk with your grandparents or other older family members about some of their memories. See if their everyday life was more influenced by their national and/or cultural traditions than yours is. Look for pictures of some of the places where your ancestors lived. Find someone in your troop, neighborhood, or school who is of the same ethnic heritage as you. Compare what you have learned with her (his, their) experiences. Share some of your findings with your troop.

3 Find a way to help your community realize and be proud of your own or someone else's cultural heritage. You might write an article for your school newspaper, prepare a neighborhood cookbook, organize a block festival, set up a library or mall exhibit, or demonstrate some dances, games, crafts, or musical specialties.

4 Create an imaginary person from a background unlike your own. Include age, sex, family and ethnic background, geographic location, job and/or education, dress, and food. Prepare a play or puppet show or write or tell a story about the character you have created.

5 Learn a language new to you. Use it in one of these ways:
   ☐ to order a meal
   ☐ as part of a skit
   ☐ to attend a language session at camp
   ☐ to help someone who speaks that language but not your own
   ☐ to design a game or word cards to help younger children learn the language

6 Go to a cultural event or festivity of an ethnic group other than your own. Take along a friend who belongs to that ethnic group, if possible. Talk to your friend or someone from the group presenting the event to learn the meaning and the background of the event. Find a way to share what you have learned with others.

OR Go to or take part in an international festival or folk fair in your locality and share your experiences with others.

7 Add your own activity here, if you wish.

My signature

Leader's signature   Date badge completed

Traveler

Complete four activities.

1 Plan a visit to the same place at least 500 km (about 300 miles) from your home for two of the people or groups below. For each person or group, plan an itinerary. Include the route to be taken, the way they will travel, and what they can see on the way and at the destination you have chosen.
   - [ ] a family that enjoys scenery
   - [ ] a sixth-grade class that wants to visit two historic sites
   - [ ] a couple who do not want to damage the environment or waste fuel
   - [ ] a Junior Girl Scout troop that enjoys camping
   - [ ] a retired naval officer who always travels by water part of the way

2 Describe to someone a week's visit to a country of your choosing. Find out about the important sights to see and things to do there. Share with your friend what you have found out about two or more aspects of the culture, such as houses, clothing, food, fine arts, crafts, music, dance, folktales, literature, languages, holidays, religions, government, political situations, history. Tell her about one or more aspects of the natural environment, such as land, flowers, trees, birds, animals.

OR Make something that will help your friend understand the country you have chosen through two or more of her senses — sight, touch, hearing, taste, or smell.

3 Design travel brochures or posters for three places in the world. One may be in the United States. Include information on what to see and do at each location.

OR Make at least one of the following for a country or culture of your choosing:
   - [ ] an article of traditional clothing
   - [ ] a folktale puppet
   - [ ] an example of a traditional craft
   - [ ] a musical instrument

Share your results with a group of younger children, telling them about the country or culture and showing them how to make something similar.

4 Pretend you are a person from another country and you have never been to the United States. Make an itinerary of what and who you would want to see in a ten-day visit. Include pictures of monuments, historic sites, and other places of interest to visit.

5 Imagine you are a travel agent and prepare the trips that will fulfill two requests listed below. For each one, except the moon trip, you will need to include where the people should go, how they will travel, and what they might see and do.

☐ "Plan a tour for me for two weeks to two islands."

☐ "Our Junior troop, which includes some girls in wheelchairs, wants to have a fun weekend nearby. Will you plan where we can go?"

☐ "I do not know where our family wants to go for our vacation. We have triplet girls, age 11. Could you plan a week filled with fun for our family?"

☐ "I want to be the first tourist on the moon. Please prepare a travel brochure that will tell me about the ride, sights, food, and where I will stay."

☐ "Where would you suggest I go on a three-day vacation? I want to know what exciting adventures you can plan for me."

6 Be part of a trip that lasts three days or more. Help in the planning. Have a special job to do during the trip. Keep a diary or log, collect postcards, take photographs, or make drawings of your travels and share them with others afterwards.

7 Add your own activity here, if you wish.

My signature

Leader's signature   Date badge completed

Wide World

Complete four activities.

1 Prepare an international exhibit that shows life around the world. It might include pictures you can find and/or models you have made of one or more of the following: houses, animals, plant life, dress, transportation, and/or markets.

2 People everywhere are proud of their nations and their heritages. Think up six questions you would like to ask a girl living outside the United States about her way of life. Find answers to at least three of your questions. Then imagine you live in this girl's country and prepare something that tells about your life and your pride in your country.

3 Take a make-believe balloon ride. Fly in your imagination over two of these areas or other places of your own choosing, far from your home:

☐ a village set high in the mountains
☐ a ship near a coral reef
☐ a desert town near oil wells
☐ a forest hideaway
☐ a river plantation in the jungle

Write a description with illustrations or make a detailed picture or 3-D construction of what you would see from the air.

4 Find out about girls in three or more of the countries in **The Wide World of Girl Guiding and Girl Scouting.** Share several activities from these countries with others. You might have a special event or teach some of the activities to someone.

5 Take a poll or survey of at least ten people you know to find out what changes they believe would make the world a better place. Share your findings with your troop.

6 Hold a meeting and/or prepare a display in your community or in your troop to inform people about the importance of a global issue and how they might do something about solving it. They might be interested in the issues of literacy, housing, water, cities, outer space, food, etc.

7 Take part in a national service project, such as New Eyes for the Needy, or in an international service project, such as Heifer Project International or International Book Project.

8 Add your own activity here, if you wish.

My signature

Leader's signature   Date badge completed

World Neighbors

Complete six activities.

1 Visit an international organization or have someone from the organization visit your troop. Places to contact might be a UNICEF center, a religious organization, a missionary office, or the local office of a women's or men's service organization that has international projects. Find out the ways in which these groups help people around the world, including people in this country.

2 Design an international scene to show life in a country outside the United States. Be sure your scene is as accurate as possible. You may want to show places where people live, work, study, worship, and/or play, along with showing what the land is like.

3 Using a recent newspaper, make a note of the names of people and places outside the United States referred to in the photos, articles, cartoons, and advertisements to find out how international your news is.

OR Listen to a news program on the radio or television and make a note of all the people and places outside the United States mentioned on the program.

For either activity, if you do not know where some of the places are located, find them in an atlas or on a world globe.

4 Start an international collection of your own, with a group of friends, or with your troop. Your collection might include stamps, songs, travel pictures, hats, flags, or recipes. Share your collection with your troop.

5 If you lived in one of the many desert or dry areas of the world, would you be able to carry water for long distances? In many places, women and girls must carry most or all the water needed in their homes each day. Try carrying a large pail nearly full of water around a block, a playing field, or a one-acre lot without spilling a drop. Then see if you can carry the container with a small amount of water in it on your head or shoulder for a short distance. Practice until you can walk with the container 3 meters (about 10 feet) without dropping it.

6 Contact someone in your community who knows about international/global issues or problems — a parent, business person, religious figure, newspaper reporter, politician, or Senior or adult Girl Scout. Talk with this person or ask her/him to speak to your troop about an important issue affecting people around the world.

7 Make something that could be used for a display to show what the world should be like for children in the year 2001.

8 Use **The Wide World of Girl Guiding and Girl Scouting** to find out about girls in various parts of the world. Do one or more of the activities in that book.

9 Think about the things you depend on someone else for and others depend on you for during a day. People almost everywhere are dependent on each other, are interdependent. Find at least three things your community or nearby communities produce for other areas and at least three items your community needs from other countries.

10 Design and carry out a small project (two hours) which will show you care about people, wherever they live.

My signature

Leader's signature   Date badge completed

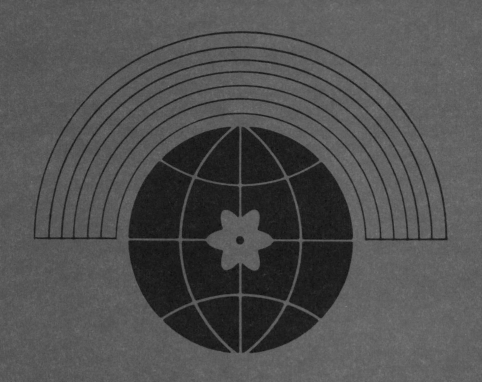

The World of
Today and Tomorrow

Dabbler

Complete one activity in each group.

A.1 Make a paper airplane that will fly in circles, turn to the left, turn to the right, and fly straight ahead. Make notes and draw or photograph your airplane so that you can build one like it whenever you want.

2 Look at three aircraft in flight or on the ground and be able to tell some of the following about each one: type of aircraft, number and kind of engines, color, identifying marks, use of aircraft, direction headed.

B.1 Take care of a plant, garden, or an animal for two weeks and keep a record of what you did, the changes you observed, and some of the things you learned.

2 Grow something in an indoor or outdoor garden that you can eat and share with your family or friends.

C.1 Write and produce a radio or television commercial advertising a product you choose. You may make up your own brand name or use a known brand.

2 Visit a corporation, bank, real estate office, or other business and find out what kind of work is done there.

D.1 Draw pictures or take photographs of energy at work in your neighborhood. (**Do not** look directly at the sun or point a camera at it.)

2 Make something that is powered by wind or water.

E.1 Be a paper engineer. Make at least two of the following out of paper: a drinking straw, a building, a bridge, a statue. Think of one other thing to build from paper and try it.

2 Make a container that will keep ice cubes from melting quickly when they are out of the refrigerator. Find out how much longer ice cubes will last in the container than without it.

F.1 Use a calculator to solve the following problems. After you do each one, turn the calculator upside down to read the word that the numbers spell. At the end you will have a sentence telling what one girl does in the summer.

	(number)	(word)
(1) $75 \times 75 - 87 =$	_____	_____
(2) $1000 \times 60 - 2265 =$	_____	_____
(3) $810 \times 710 + 2245 =$	_____	_____
(4) $150{,}000 \div 3 + 7738 =$	_____	_____
(5) $3550 \div 5 =$	_____	_____
(6) $1327 \times 40 =$	_____	_____

2 Find out at least two of the following in metric units:
- ☐ how tall you are
- ☐ how much you weigh
- ☐ how far you travel one way to school
- ☐ how long your foot is

G.1 Find something that needs to be repaired and fix it yourself or help someone else fix it.

2 Show someone how to take care of a bicycle: how to lubricate it with oil or silicone, pump up a tire, raise or lower the seat and handlebars, and adjust the kickstand.

H.1 Make silver polish by adding a small amount of lemon juice to cream of tartar. Mix together with a spoon until you have a paste. Then use a little of this paste on a cloth to clean tarnished silver by rubbing. After the tarnish is gone, rinse the piece of silver in water and shine it with a soft towel or cloth. If you can't find any silver to polish, try an old quarter or dime.

2 Visit a science museum, planetarium, observatory, weather station, or laboratory. Ask questions about things you see.

I.1 Make up a skit to show you know how to send emergency messages by telephone, CB radio, signaling, or other means.

2 Fingerprint yourself and the members of your family and notice any similarities or differences.

J.1 Make marbleized paper, try a crayon-resist, or dye something using a batik method

  2 Try to remove spots or stains with water from three or more surfaces, such as wood, linoleum, metal, or glass. You may add cleaning aids to the water to help you. Notice what kinds of spots are easy to remove and which cleaning aids work best for which spots.

My signature

Leader's signature   Date badge completed

Aerospace

Complete six activities, including the one starred.

*1 Put together a simple model glider or make your own out of balsa wood. See if you can make your glider fly straight, stall, loop, bank right, bank left.

2 Invite someone who is involved with aerospace (astronomy, aviation, or space) to tell your troop about her/his job or flying experiences and the future of aerospace.

OR Talk to some older people in your community about what it was like to fly in the first half of the 20th century. You might ask about: early aircraft, barnstorming, dirigibles, coast-to-coast travel, Amelia Earhart, Powder Puff Derby, and military flying in the two world wars. Share what you find out.

3 See a space launch in person, on television, or in a movie. Keep a record of your observations including:
☐ date and place of launch
☐ country and origin of space vehicle or satellite
☐ kind of space vehicle or satellite
☐ purpose of launch and whether it was successful
☐ something new learned from the mission

OR Visit an airport, a control tower, a space center, an aerospace museum, or a planetarium, or see an air show.

4 Look through a telescope at three or more heavenly objects, such as a star cluster, a nebula, a galaxy, a planet, a moon.

OR Observe three or more of the following with the unaided eye: a planet, a double star, a meteor, an almost new moon, a star cluster, a galaxy.

5 Make and fly your own kite. Experiment with it to find out which winds are best and how to make the kite fly better.

6 Put on an air show and invite other groups to participate.
- ☐ Have races for different kinds of model aircraft, such as gliders and airplanes, with awards for different achievements, such as longest flight, best stunt, most accurate flight.
- ☐ Have a kite-flying contest.

7 Create your own comic book, television, or science fiction character who uses flight in her/his job. Describe the character by providing the following information in a way you choose:
- ☐ the name of your character
- ☐ why flight is necessary for your character
- ☐ how flight is accomplished by your character
- ☐ how your character feels when she/he flies
- ☐ what your character wears

8 Make an aerospace mobile from inexpensive materials, such as coat hangers, construction paper or cardboard, and thread. Include at least one piece of information that has been discovered about astronomy or space in your lifetime.

9 Take a person or group outside to show her/him the Big Dipper and North Star (if these are visible in your area) and four other constellations. Learn the names of some of the bright stars in the constellations.

10 Find pictures of or actually collect five or more postage stamps that have something to do with aerospace.

OR Design your own postage stamp to commemorate an aerospace event or person.

11 Suppose that thinking beings have been found in space and an unmanned spaceship can reach them. Choose ten items to send them that would tell about present-day life on earth and show that we are friendly beings contacting them in peace. Describe the items and tell why you chose them.

My signature

Leader's signature   Date badge completed

Business-Wise

Complete four activities, including the one starred.

*1 Think about a business you could really start now by yourself or with others, or one that you might be interested in starting in the future. Make a business plan that tells:

☐ what product you will make or what service you will provide
☐ who your customers will be
☐ the name of your business
☐ how you will get the money or supplies to start the business
☐ who will be responsible for which job
☐ how you will make your product or provide your service
☐ how much you will charge for your product or service
☐ how you will find the right place to locate your business and get your product or service to the customers
☐ how you will advertise your product or service
☐ how you will keep accurate records of income and expenses

2 If possible, take part in running the business you thought about, according to your business plan for at least a month.

OR Carry out the advertising part of your business plan.

3 Show the way you will present yourself and your product or service to your customers. You could do this by showing you know how to use correct business manners when you meet customers, when you speak to them on the telephone, or when you write them a business letter.

4 Find out about opening a savings or checking account for a business, about the services offered by the bank, the amount of interest the bank pays, and how the bank uses its money.

5 Invite someone in business to talk to your troop.

OR Visit a business and find out what goes on there.

6 Watch a film or television program on economics or business and share what you find out.

7 Use the profits (if any) from your business to carry out a project that will benefit others.

8 Write your own activity here, if you wish.

My signature

Leader's signature   Date badge completed

Computer Fun

Complete six activities.

1 Look through books, newspapers, or magazines, watch television, and/or go in person to find computers being used for at least five different purposes. Share what you find with your troop members.

2 Spend half an hour or more learning something from a computer either through Computer Assisted Instruction (CAI) at a school or learning center or by using a computer educational toy.

3 Find out the names of at least three computer languages. In one of these, learn the symbols you would use to get the computer to add, subtract, multiply, and divide.

4 Help put on a demonstration of computer toys and games for your troop.

5 Visit a business, bank, or other place that uses a computer to solve problems.
   ☐ See the computer in action and find out some of the things it is used for.
   ☐ Find out what language the computer uses, how information is put in, and how information comes out.

OR Invite someone who works with computers to talk to your troop. Find out what she/he does with the computer, what training was necessary, and what other people are involved in keeping the computer working.

6 Find a place, such as a high school or business that has a keypunch machine for punching computer cards. Watch someone punch information on the card or punch one yourself with your name, address, and phone number on it. Find out how the letters and numbers are related to the positions of the holes on the card.

OR See and find out about another kind of input for a computer, such as a light pen, disc, magnetic tape, typing, video, or other terminal. Share what you find out.

7 Find a calculator game or puzzle book. Choose three games or puzzles. Use a calculator to find the answers. Try out the games or puzzles on your friends.

8 Use a calculator to find out whether it would be more profitable for you to take a job paying $500 a month or one paying 1 cent the first day, 2 cents the second day, 4 cents the third day, and so on, doubling the salary each day for the 30-day month.

9 Spend half an hour or more playing an electronic computer game. Keep a record of how you do.

10 Think up a computer or computerized robot you would like to have.
   ☐ What would it look like?
   ☐ What would you name it?
   ☐ What would you program it to do?
   ☐ Describe your computer to someone in words or a picture.

OR Read a science fiction book about computers or robots and tell someone about the story.

11 Show that you know how to count in the binary number system (base two), the way computers do, by deciphering the following binary message (see instructions below).

First Word   00111   01111   01111   00100

Second Word   10011   01000   01111   10111

Third Word   11001   01111   10101   10010   00101

Fourth Word   00001

Fifth Word   10000   10010   01111

To decipher the message:
a. First, change each binary number to a decimal number. Instead of the ones, tens, hundreds, thousands, etc. used as place names in the decimal system (base ten), the binary system (base two) uses ones, twos, fours, eights, sixteens, etc., to mark its places. The binary number 01101 equals 13 in the decimal system. Here's why:

16	8	4	2	1	Binary place names
0	1	1	0	1	Binary number

Reading the chart on page 83 from right to left, we see:

one 1	$1 \times 1 = 1$
no 2s	$0 \times 2 = 0$
one 4	$1 \times 4 = 4$
one 8	$1 \times 8 = 8$
no 16s	$0 \times 16 = \underline{0}$
	13

Adding the above, we get 13 in the decimal system.

b. After you change each binary number in the message to a decimal number, substitute the corresponding letter of the alphabet. In the example given above, the letter would be M because that is the 13th letter of the alphabet. Thus M corresponds to the binary number 01101.

12 Write your own activity here, if you wish.

My signature

Leader's signature   Date badge completed

Do-It-Yourself

Complete four activities.

1 Have a troop carwash or wash and/or wax your family's or a neighbor's car or truck. Clean the inside as well as the outside of the car.

2 Find out the names and uses for two or more tools in each of these categories: measuring, cutting, fastening, and striking. Help make a repair on a bicycle, skateboard, or a toy using a fastening tool.

3 Spend several days helping with outdoor work around a home or yard. Some things you might do are mowing or watering the lawn, raking leaves, shoveling snow, painting, repairing or moving outdoor furniture, and mending broken screens or fences. Keep a record of what you do.

4 Watch a house or building being put up in your town or a wall or foundation being built. Observe the work on several different days. Find out as much as you can about what is being done and keep a record of what you see.

5 Visit a lumberyard or home supply store or talk to a building contractor or mason to find out about some of the following:
- ☐ the difference between cement, concrete, and mortar
- ☐ the different uses of gravel mix, mortar mix, and sand mix
- ☐ the different kinds of lumber and their uses
- ☐ the kinds of tools masons use
- ☐ the depth of the frost line in your location and why it is important to know it
- ☐ the reason for holes in concrete blocks and bricks
- ☐ the order in which the parts of a building are built
- ☐ the kinds of earth-moving equipment and heavy machinery used in putting up buildings

Share what you find out.

6 Show that you know how to do three or more of the following things to a car or truck:

☐ Check the liquid level in the radiator and add water or antifreeze, if needed.

☐ Check the oil level and add the right kind and amount of oil, if needed.

☐ Check the liquid level in the battery and add the right kind and amount of water, if needed.

☐ Check the air in the tires and add or remove the right amount of air, if needed.

☐ Check the liquid in the windshield washer bottle and add the right kind and amount of liquid, if needed.

7 Have someone tell you about five or more kinds of wood joints or look at pictures of them in a do-it-yourself book. Make an inspection tour where you live or where your troop meets and try to find as many different kinds of wood joints as you can. You might look at the back of drawers, at a wooden box, table, chair, or picture frame, or at the molding on a door or window. Share what you find. Then make something that has a wood joint or cut a piece of wood using a miter box.

8 Do one or more of the following:

☐ Help change a washer in a leaky faucet.

☐ Help paint or refinish a piece of furniture.

☐ Help fix a crack or hole in a wall or sidewalk.

☐ Help with some painting, papering, or other repair work.

9 Make a solar cooker and use it to cook a hot dog or some other food.

10 Write your own activity here, if you wish.

My signature

Leader's signature   Date badge completed

Energy
Saver

Complete six activities, including the one starred.

*1 Find three or more ways you can save energy in your home, meeting place, or school. Talk over your plans with your family and troop members or invite an energy expert to talk to your troop to get more ideas. Then actually use one or more of the ideas to save energy.

2 Make up a game about people, places, or things connected with energy and play it with others.

3 Take a tour of a power plant used by your utility company to produce electricity for your community.

OR Visit a place that uses wind, solar, geothermal, or some other energy source in a new way to make heat or electricity.

For either choice, show what you found out. Try to include energy-saving ideas.

4 Do a troop, family, or individual recycling project.

OR Make a source of fuel for a fireplace or campfire by rolling your own paper logs (see instructions below). Burn at least one paper log to find out how long it will burn and how much heat it will give.

To roll your own paper logs:

a. Take an old broomstick handle and roll a sheet of newspaper around it.

b. Continue rolling sheets of paper, one on top of the other.

c. When the paper logs are 10 cm (about 4 in.) thick, tie the rolled bundle of newspaper with a piece of wire near each end and remove from broom.

5 Collect some stories and pictures about the different kinds of energy being considered to help our country supply its own energy needs. Share your findings.

6 Find out about ways energy was made and used in your community over 50 years ago. You might do one or more of the following:

☐ Interview older people about energy sources they used in the past.

☐ Visit a site where energy was made or used, such as an old coal mine, grist mill, or oil well.

☐ Invite a speaker from your public utility company to tell you how energy was made in the past.

Share what you find out.

7 Make a draftometer and test your home, school, or meeting place for air leakage (see instructions below).

Have someone show you what is available to close air leaks around windows and doors. Try to do something about the leaks.

To make a draftometer:

a. Cut a 12 cm by 25 cm (approximately 5 in. by 10 in.) strip of plastic food wrap.

b. Tape the strip to a long pencil so that the plastic hangs freely.

c. Blow the plastic gently and notice how it reacts to air.

d. Test for air leakage by holding the draftometer near the edges of closed windows and doors.

8 Make and use a solar still (see instructions below). Let the still work for at least four hours, then taste the water in the cup. (Check the still every hour, if you can.) Think of two or more uses for a solar still.

To make a solar still:

a. Fill a deep cooking pan to a depth of 2.5 cm (about 1 in.) with some salty water that you make yourself and place the pan near a sunny window or outside on a sunny day. (A pan with a dark inside surface works best.)

b. Put a teacup or small glass right side up in the middle of the pan.

c. Cover the pan with clear plastic and tape the plastic securely.

d. Put a rock or weight on the plastic wrap to make it sag in the middle over the cup, but don't let the rock or plastic touch the cup.

OR Make and test some simple solar hot air collectors (see instructions below). When you are finished, tell someone two or more important things to think about when building solar hot air collectors.

To make and test solar hot air collectors:

a. Take two shallow metal cake pans and put a piece of white construction paper in one and a black piece in the other.

b. Put three or four ice cubes in one pan and the same number in the other.

c. Quickly put some clear plastic food wrap over each pan, secure with a rubber band or tape, and place both pans in a sunny south window or outside on a sunny day.

d. Notice which ice cubes melt faster.

e. Now repeat steps a through d, but this time use black construction paper in both pans and tilt one pan toward the sun.

9 Find out how heat and hot water are made in your home, school, meeting place, or other building. Look at the furnace or boiler room if possible. Find out about the kind of insulation being used to keep heat from escaping too quickly. Share what you find out, including some energy-saving ideas.

10 Show two or more ways to do each of the following:

☐ Keep comfortable when the temperature is above 28°C (82°F) without air conditioning or an electric fan.

☐ Keep comfortable when the temperature is below 18°C (64°F) without turning up the thermostat or using electricity.

☐ Travel without using fossil fuels, such as gasoline, kerosene, coal, and diesel fuel.

My signature

Leader's signature   Date badge completed

Food Raiser

Complete four activities, including the one starred.

*1 On paper, design an outdoor garden that includes at least three vegetables your family or friends will eat. Find out about companion planting, how to keep tall plants from shading smaller ones, where to start the garden, and other things you should know. Use this information to help you in your design.

2 Do a soil test on a lawn or garden or have it done to find out how good the soil is, whether or not it will grow vegetables, flowers, and grass, and which nutrients, such as fertilizer, lime, and humus, the soil needs. When you get the results, help improve the soil.

OR Describe one or more ways farmers and ranchers do each of the following:
   ☐ Keep topsoil from being blown or washed away.
   ☐ Prevent overgrazing of grasslands.
   ☐ Keep soil from becoming too poor for growing crops.

3 Plant and care for a garden according to the design you made. Keep a record of how you prepared the soil; when you planted and harvested each crop; how often you watered, weeded, and added fertilizer; how you kept out pests; and ideas of how you could improve your garden another year. Harvest each crop at the proper time and share it with others.

4 For at least two weeks take care of an animal, such as a chicken, rabbit, or lamb, that is usually raised for food. Keep a daily record of what you did.

OR If you cannot take care of a real animal that is usually raised for food, choose one you would like to raise. Record how you would take care of this animal for two weeks. Include the kind and amount of food, feeding schedules, where your animal would live, how it would get its exercise, and special health problems of this animal.

5 Go fishing for fresh water fish, salt water fish, or shellfish.
   ☐ Learn the names of the fish you are trying to catch and get a fishing permit if you need one.
   ☐ Get the right kind of bait, line, and/or other equipment. Help clean, cook, and eat some of the fish you catch.

OR Choose a body of water located near your home, if possible.

☐ Find out what kind of fish are found and caught there during different seasons of the year and if any fish or other foods are harvested from this body of water for commercial use.

☐ Exhibit your findings.

☐ Eat some fish or other food from this body of water if you can.

6 In a medium other than soil, such as water, gravel, or wood chips, grow something that you can eat.

7 Spend several days living and working on a farm or ranch, either on your own or with your family or troop. Learn about life there by helping with the work and by asking questions about what you see. Keep a daily journal of your experiences.

OR If you live on a farm or ranch, invite some girls who do not live on one to visit you. Help them experience what your life is like by showing them around, by explaining what they see, and by letting them help you.

8 Imagine that you are a nutrition expert who knows the importance of soybeans as a good source of protein and calcium, as well as other vitamins and minerals. Your job is to convince the people who think soybeans are unappetizing and dull that they really are delicious as well as nutritious. Have a soybean tasting party. Make your own soybean snacks to convince others that soybeans are good to eat.

9 Talk to the county cooperative extension agent and/or some farmers, ranchers, and people in the fishing business in your own county or in the closest rural county to learn about agriculture or fishing in your area.

OR Invite someone to talk to you about the part agriculture plays in a developing country.

For either choice, share what you find out.

10 Write your own activity here, if you wish.

My signature

Leader's signature   Date badge completed

Foods, Fibers, and Farming

Complete six activities.

1 Try your hand at food processing. Make butter, cheese, yogurt, raisins, applesauce, or a processed food of your own choice.

2 Tour a farm, ranch, aquafarm, or agribusiness. Ask questions about the things that interest you. After the visit, describe what you saw, heard, felt, smelled, and/or tasted.

3 Grow sprouts from mung bean, alfalfa, or other seeds that sprout, to eat in salads or sandwiches or as a side dish.

4 Grow a vegetable that you like to eat. If space is limited, choose a mini-vegetable like cherry tomatoes. Care for your vegetable properly and, when it is ripe, prepare and eat it.

5 Go to a county fair or other exhibit on agriculture. Find out two or more things about foods, fibers, or farming that you didn't know before and the names and uses for two or more pieces of heavy farm equipment. Share what you find out.

6 Visit a food or fiber processing plant. Learn all you can about the steps involved in getting something from the field to you as a finished product. You might visit a:
- ☐ cannery
- ☐ flour mill
- ☐ cereal plant
- ☐ feed or meal company
- ☐ frozen food processing plant
- ☐ wool or cotton mill
- ☐ citrus processing plant
- ☐ meat, fish, or poultry packing company

7 Visit a veterinarian or invite one to come to a troop meeting. Find out about the work she/he does. Does this person work with farm animals as well as with people's pets? Find out what it takes to become a veterinarian.

8 Show in a way of your choosing how you would have done at least
   two of the following on a farm or ranch in the early 1800s, how you
   would do them today, and how you might do them in the 21st century:
   ☐ plow a field
   ☐ harvest a crop
   ☐ cook a meal
   ☐ milk a cow
   ☐ make clothes
   ☐ graze the animals
   ☐ round up the animals
   ☐ get food for the animals

9 Find or describe three weeds or three insects that cause problems to
   farmers or gardeners in your area. Identify each pest by name and
   describe the kind of problem it causes, and how you can get rid of it
   (without using chemical pesticides, if possible).

OR Describe three insects that are helpful to farmers or gardeners in
   your area and tell how each one helps.

10 Visit a place where water plants or animals are being raised for food
   or fertilizer, or for ornamentation or jewelry.

OR Visit a store or market where fresh food is sold. Find out where the
   fresh food comes from, how it gets to market, how it is kept fresh, and
   other steps in its travels from its beginning until you buy it.

   For either choice, share what you find out.

My signature

Leader's signature   Date badge completed

Math Whiz

Complete six activities.

1 Find a math puzzle book. Choose three puzzles and figure out the answers. Try the puzzles on your friends.

OR Perform three card tricks that use mathematical or logical thinking. Have the group try to guess how you know the answers.

2 Play the game of Nim several times with another person. Try to figure out how to win every time. To play:

a. Put nine pennies in three rows, with four pennies in one row, three in the next, and two in the last row.

b. The two players take turns removing pennies, using these rules: A player can take away pennies from only one row during a turn. The player can take as many pennies as she likes from the row, but must take at least one.

c. The player who takes the last penny is the winner.

3 Think up a prediction, such as, "I think that one out of every five people walking down Main Street between two and three o'clock will be wearing jeans."

☐ Make up a plan to check out your prediction, then carry it out.

☐ Compare your prediction with the results.

4 Make a symmetrical design using geometric figures in needlepoint, cross-stitch, embroidery, knitting, crocheting, or patchwork.

OR Make a string design that gives the feeling of curves but uses only straight pieces of thread. Mount your string design on a board using nails that have small, flat heads.

5 Suppose pizza is your favorite snack and your favorite pizza parlor has it with four different kinds of topping (pepperoni, sausage, peppers, or mushrooms):

☐ How many pizzas would you have to buy if you wanted all possible combinations using only two toppings per pizza?

☐ Suppose the pizza parlor has five different kinds of topping. Now, how many pizzas would you have to buy to get all possible combinations, still using only two toppings per pizza?

☐ Answer the same question for other numbers of toppings.

6 Read a mystery story, watch a television or movie mystery, or play a game of **Clue.**

☐ As you notice clues that you think will lead to the solution, write them down.

☐ If you guess the solution before the book or movie tells you or if you win the game of **Clue,** figure out how you did it.

☐ If you didn't guess the solution ahead of time, go over the clues again to see how they lead you to the solution.

7 Show how to send and receive messages in at least one kind of code or cipher and one kind of invisible ink.

8 Play a strategy game, such as chess, checkers, or three-dimensional tic-tac-toe with one or more people until you win at least one game. Try to figure out the best moves to make to outsmart the person you are playing against.

9 Have a contest to find out who can calculate most accurately how many objects of a similar size can fit into a large container.

☐ Choose the container and the objects, such as popcorn or marbles.

☐ Let the contestants measure the container and a small number of the objects and then calculate their answer.

☐ Give an award to the winner(s).

My signature

Leader's signature   Date badge completed

Ms. Fix-It

Complete six activities.

1 Learn about nails and other material fasteners with some members of your troop. Each person should bring in one kind of nail and one kind of other material fastener, such as a screw or bolt, to show the others.
   - ☐ Each of you should tell the group the names of the objects you brought and what they are used for.
   - ☐ Put all the objects in a box, mix them up, and have a contest to see who can identify the most.
   - ☐ During the following week find three or more places where nails and other material fasteners are used and share what you find with troop members.

2 Visit a hardware store or someone's workshop and find out about:
   - ☐ the names and uses of some of the tools
   - ☐ how to handle and store the tools safely
   - ☐ some of the other things you see there

3 Make something out of wood that involves boring one or more holes, using nails or other types of material fasteners, and measuring and cutting the wood.

4 Invite a plumber, mason, carpenter, electrician, heating engineer, repair person, or auto or bicycle mechanic to your troop meeting to tell you about her/his work and show you some of the tools used on the job, or watch one of these people at work and ask questions about what you see.

5 Show and name the tools you would use to:
   - ☐ cut glass
   - ☐ spread putty
   - ☐ mend a crack in plaster
   - ☐ paint a room
   - ☐ square a corner
   - ☐ level a table

6 Find out what the dials and lights on a car, truck, or bus dashboard mean.
   - [ ] What do they look like when they are in their normal positions?
   - [ ] How can you tell if something is wrong?
   - [ ] What should you do if you notice something wrong?

7 Find out what to do, whom to call, which switch to push, or which handle to turn in three or more of the following emergencies:
   - [ ] water won't stop running in a sink or toilet
   - [ ] something goes wrong with the furnace
   - [ ] something goes wrong with the hot water heater
   - [ ] toilet gets clogged
   - [ ] thermostat won't shut off/turn on furnace
   - [ ] smoke alarm or security system won't shut off after emergency is over
   - [ ] gas is leaking in the kitchen or other part of the house

8 Have someone show you what to do if the lights go out while you are home alone.
   - [ ] Look at the electrical panel box where you live, if possible.
   - [ ] Find out about fuses and circuit breakers and how to change or reset them.
   - [ ] Find out how to turn off the electricity in case of flood, fire, or other emergency.
   - [ ] Show that you can change a light bulb.
   - [ ] Show that you know three or more safety rules to follow when using electricity.

9 Use one or more carpenter's tools to fix something that needs repairing.

10 Repair something with one or more of the following: nails, tacks, screws, bolts, staples, screw eyes, wire, electrician's tape, putty, caulking material, glue.

My signature

Leader's signature   Date badge completed

Putting Things Together

Complete six activities, including the one starred.

*1 Look up "engineer" in the yellow pages of the telephone book and make a list of all the different kinds of engineers you see there.

OR Ask people what kinds of engineers there are until you find at least five different kinds.

For either choice, find out what at least three kinds of engineers do in their jobs.

2 Show at least eight things you see or use during a day that wouldn't be there if there were no engineers.

3 Put together a jigsaw puzzle that has at least 100 pieces. Try to figure out where the pieces fit by looking at them carefully before you try them.

4 Find out the size of a court used for tennis, handball, jai alai, basketball, paddle tennis, or other sport. Make a scale drawing of the one you choose.

OR Make a scale drawing of a three-dimensional object, such as a box or can. Show a side view, a top view, and a front view on the same piece of paper.

5 Figure out a way you can show that moving an object by rolling it is easier than pushing it. Find two or more useful ways an engineer uses this idea.

6 With a model construction set build at least one of the models suggested in the directions that come with the set and two other models of your own choosing.

OR Invent and/or make a simple machine and use it to do something useful.

7 Draw or take pictures of the bridges in your area. For each bridge find out:
- ☐ what the bridge is used for
- ☐ what type of bridge it is
- ☐ what material it is made from

OR Make a model of a bridge, such as a drawbridge or suspension, arch, pontoon, or cantilever bridge.

8 Have a materials hunt in your neighborhood. Bring back the name, description, and location of something made out of each of the following materials:

brick	paper
cement	plastic
cinder block	sheetrock
concrete	stone
marble	wood
metal	

9 Make and test a simple beam support (see instructions below). Look around your home or community to find at least two examples of beam supports at work.

To make and test a simple beam support:

a. Take a piece of cardboard about 30 cm (12 in.) long and 2.5 cm (1 in.) wide.

b. Fasten the cardboard strip down on a table by putting a heavy book on it, allowing 20 cm (8 in.) of cardboard to stick out over the edge of the table.

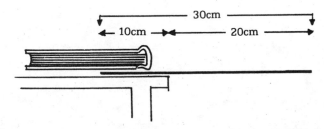

c. Put pennies, one on top of another, near the end of the cardboard farthest from the edge of the table until no more pennies will stay on. Write down the number of pennies.

d. Now cut two strips of cardboard, one 25 cm (10 in.) long and 2.5 cm (1 in.) wide and the other 15 cm (6 in.) long and 2.5 cm (1 in.) wide to make the beam support.

e. Tape these two strips of cardboard to the piece of cardboard sticking out over the edge of the table to support the beam like this:

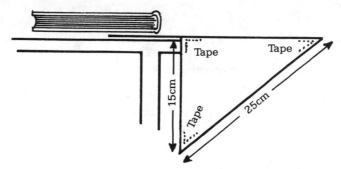

Be sure the 15 cm (6 in.) piece is securely taped to the 30 cm (12 in.) piece of cardboard at the point where they meet at the edge of the table.

f. Now pile up the pennies near the end of the beam as you did before. How many pennies will it hold this time?

10 Visit a manufacturing plant or factory where something is being put together. Look for examples of how machines and robots are used.

11 Have an engineer show and explain to you a drawing, blueprint, or plan of something she/he is working on. Ask the person to tell you about some of the exciting projects or products engineers are working on for a better tomorrow.

12 Create a structure using small sticks or other material of your choice. Make it artistic and sturdy. Tell how you used your knowledge of art and science to build the structure.

My signature

Leader's signature   Date badge completed

Science
Around
Town

Complete four activities.

1 Invite a firefighter, police officer, or emergency medical technician to your troop meeting or visit one or more of them at work to find out how they use science and technology in their jobs. Share what you discover with others.

2 Talk to some senior citizens to find out how science and technology have changed their way of life. Some of the things you might ask are:
☐ how they traveled when they were your age
☐ how they cooked
☐ who made their clothes and what the material was like
☐ how they heated and lighted their homes
☐ how they kept cool in hot weather
☐ how they found out about what was going on in the world
☐ what their appliances looked like
☐ how they communicated with friends and relatives in other towns or cities

Show how things have changed during the 20th century or some of the ways you think things will change in the 21st century.

3 Find out how two or more short and/or long distance communication devices, such as a computerized telephone, a picture phone, a telegraph, a teletype machine, a personal paging device (beeper), or a communication satellite work.

4 Choose a product of technology that you use or have heard about and find out how it works — not just how to turn it on or use it, but what goes on inside. Some examples you might enjoy finding out about are:
☐ a television set
☐ a smoke or fire detector
☐ a home security system
☐ a video disc player or an audio or video cassette recorder
☐ an electric automobile
☐ an electronic checkout register at a supermarket

Look at the inside of the product, if you can. Share what you find out.

5 Find out the ways in which your community is using technology to help meet the needs of the disabled, such as providing telephones for the deaf or special buses for those in wheelchairs. Talk to some disabled people to find out some of their needs and suggestions. Talk to some engineers, scientists, and community leaders to find out what they are doing to meet those needs. Share what you find out with your troop, make some suggestions for future community efforts, and try to carry out one of your ideas.

6 Find out by talking to people who work with computers and/or by visiting places where they are used, how they are used in at least one of the following fields: transportation, banking and other business, or communication. Share what you find out.

7 Design a transportation system for a city or country in the 21st century.

OR Design something using science and technology that you would like to have in your community in the near future to improve the quality of life.

8 Write your own activity here, if you wish.

My signature

Leader's signature   Date badge completed

Science in Action

Complete six activities.

1 With the help of a police officer or other person, lift a fingerprint or make a mold of a footprint or tire track. Find out some of the ways police departments use computers and other new equipment in solving crimes.

2 Visit your local emergency service. Look around inside the ambulance. Find out about the equipment. Learn the emergency telephone number.

3 Find out how science and technology help fire fighters. Visit a firehouse or ask a fire fighter:
   ☐ how a pressure nozzle works
   ☐ what protective clothing is made of and what kind is available
   ☐ how the fire alarm box works and what other types of communication are used
   ☐ what tools are used in a fire fighter's work
   ☐ how at least one type of fire extinguisher works, the chemicals it contains, and the kinds of fires it will put out

4 For two days, make a list of all the things you use that are electric. Next to these things, write down what you would have used if you had lived 100 years ago. Describe what you think one of these things might be like 100 years from now.

5 Listen to at least three of the following types of radio broadcasts or transmissions in your home or community and find out who is allowed to broadcast or transmit, what frequency is used, and what the letters stand for.
   ☐ AM broadcast
   ☐ FM broadcast
   ☐ CB transmission
   ☐ foreign shortwave broadcast
   ☐ Voice of America broadcast
   ☐ ham radio transmission
   ☐ maritime mobile and marine transmission
   ☐ police, fire, public service/emergency broadcast
   ☐ commercial radio transmission

6 Visit a photo lab, printing plant, Coast Guard station, radio or television station, telephone switching center, satellite tracking station, factory, food processing plant, or other place where machines and technical equipment are being used. Share what you find out.

7 Take a ride on a passenger train, rapid transit system, long-distance bus, or commercial aircraft with your troop or family. Have a contest to see who can discover the most ways that science and technology help make your trip safer, speedier, and happier from the time you buy your ticket until you reach your destination. Learn a railroad song or other travel song.

8 Show that you know how to use two or more automatic machines, such as a pay telephone, change machine, stamp machine, exact change toll machine, parking meter, coin or ticket operated turnstile, or other vending machine. Know what to do if you lose your money in the machine. If possible, have someone open one of the machines and show you how it works.

9 Take a trip to the water purification plant in your town or city and find out where the water comes from, how it is purified, and what equipment is used.

OR If your house uses well water, find out what scientific tests are used to be sure the water is safe to drink, how often these tests are performed, and the kind of chemicals that are added to the water. Test the water if you can.

10 See an exhibit about a city of the future or read a story about such a city and share what you find out.

OR Create a drawing of what you imagine that a city of the future might be like. Include things like transportation, communication, and other services that people will need.

My signature

Leader's signature   Date badge completed

Science Sleuth

Complete six activities, including the one starred.

*1 Do at least one thing an astronomer, chemist, geologist, meteorologist, oceanographer, or physicist might do in her/his work.

- [ ] Look at some stars and planets through a telescope or identify five constellations.
- [ ] Test household products to find out whether they are acids or bases.
- [ ] Collect and identify five rocks and minerals or visit a place of geological interest in your area.
- [ ] Make a barometer, wind vane, wind speed indicator, or rain gauge and use it to record the weather for a week.
- [ ] Find out if things float better in salt water or in fresh water.
- [ ] Make a battery or turn a nail into an electromagnet.
- [ ] Think up your own project.

2 Make a simple musical instrument that you can tune. Listen to the pitch of the sound and try ways to change the pitch.

- [ ] Try to explain how the sound is made.
- [ ] Play a simple melody.

3 View an eclipse of the moon, a meteor shower, a comet, or the northern lights. Make a record of what you saw and how you felt.

4 Figure out ways to do two of the following and show someone else how to do them:

- [ ] Move water from one jar to another without pouring.
- [ ] Make a fire extinguisher and put out a fire.
- [ ] Show that air exerts pressure.
- [ ] Send and read messages written with invisible ink.
- [ ] Make something float that is heavier than water.

5 Keep a record of the kinds of clouds you see at the same time each day for a week and the kind of weather that goes with them. Figure out a theory about how clouds and weather are related and check it out during another week.

OR Visit a weather station and find out how the instruments work.

6 Grow crystals out of sugar, salt, or another substance. Find out the chemical names and formulas of the substances you are working with. Look at the crystals with a magnifying glass and describe what you see.

7 Invite a physical scientist to talk to your troop or visit one in her/his laboratory. Find out about the scientist's work and about some new things that are happening in her/his field.

8 Search for clues in your community or in a place you visit that show one or more of the following:

☐ a glacier has been there
☐ a volcano has been active in the past
☐ erosion has taken place
☐ water once covered the area
☐ the earth has shifted
☐ intense heat has been present
☐ strong winds, tides, or currents have affected the area

Make a record of your clues.

9 Choose a measurement, such as length, volume, mass (weight), or temperature and make a poster that shows the metric units for that measurement. Use it to teach someone the metric system.

10 See the show at a planetarium or laserium.

11 Look around your home and community to find at least one example of each of the six simple machines: the inclined plane, the lever, the pulley, the screw, the wedge, and the wheel and axle. Share your examples.

12 Observe waves in motion. You might make a wave bottle (see instructions below). Then, do one of the following to get waves of sound or light to work for you:

☐ Make sound louder (you might make a megaphone).
☐ Make sound carry farther (you might make a string telephone).
☐ Make light brighter and hotter (you might safely burn a hole in paper, using a magnifying glass).

To make a wave bottle:

a. Fill a clear, colorless bottle with one-half mineral oil and one-half rubbing alcohol.

b. Add several drops of food coloring to the liquid in the bottle.

c. Cap the bottle tightly.

Make waves by rocking the bottle back and forth.

My signature

Leader's signature   Date badge completed

Water Wonders

Complete six activities, including the one starred.

*1 Look at a globe, a world map, or a picture of earth taken from space to see why earth is called the water planet. Find out what H_2O means and give three good reasons why nothing can live without it. Share your answers after you've thought about the following:
- ☐ being thirsty or dirty
- ☐ a nice day after a good rain
- ☐ the things we get from the waters of earth
- ☐ the many ways we depend on water

2 Compare the difference between salt water and fresh water. Do at least one experiment to find out which:
- ☐ boils first
- ☐ freezes first
- ☐ yields salt crystals
- ☐ makes better soapsuds
- ☐ makes floating easier

3 Find out ways that water carries things and leaves them behind. Do at least one of the following:
- ☐ Shake up a jar of water with some gravel, sand, silt, and clay. Watch which settles first and how layers of sediment form.
- ☐ Look for fossils of water life in nature or in things made of stone (for example, in buildings, tables, etc.).
- ☐ Trace the "waterways" inside plants and animals. Explain how food and other life-needs are carried by sap and blood.
- ☐ Look closely along a shoreline for debris, such as shells, pebbles, plants, bottles, and decaying matter. Figure out where it came from, how it got there, and what is likely to happen to it.
- ☐ Find out what causes cloudiness in water. You may need to use a filter, a plankton net, a magnifying glass, or even a microscope.

4 Look at things that live underwater. Visit a place like an aquarium, set up your own aquarium, or make a waterscope to help you observe a water habitat. Choose at least three of the following and figure out how or why:

- ☐ some kinds of water life move
- ☐ some kinds of water life stay in one place
- ☐ most fish have light-colored bellies and dark-colored backs
- ☐ some fish swim in schools
- ☐ some water creatures have shells or can close themselves up
- ☐ some forms of water life live under or on the bottom, some in the middle, and some on the surface of the water

5 Carefully watch at least two of the following:

- ☐ things floating with a current or in a whirlpool
- ☐ the flow or drip from a faucet or hose
- ☐ ripples in a pool or waves along a shore
- ☐ the rise and fall of the tide

Then use water in motion to do two of the following:

- ☐ Have a race with floating objects like leaves or toy boats.
- ☐ Measure tidal differences and check them with a tide table.
- ☐ Handle a boat safely in waves or a current.
- ☐ Swim safely in waves or a current.
- ☐ Learn how a toilet works.
- ☐ Collect and measure the amount of water that would be wasted if you let a faucet drip for an hour.

6 Try one of the following float tests:

- ☐ Make a floating toy and try it out in a bathtub or pool.
- ☐ Show how to fall into water and float with your clothes on.
- ☐ Test PFDs (Personal Flotation Devices) for fit and see how they help you float.

7 Look closely at places where land and water meet. Do at least one of the following:

- ☐ Measure water depths. Mark shallow areas where it's safe to wade or deep areas where it's safe to dive.
- ☐ Dig and sculpt clay or sand into an imaginary water creature.
- ☐ Look for living things that burrow in mud or sand.
- ☐ Cast animal tracks you find by the water's edge.
- ☐ Find out how to tell a good place to anchor a boat.

8 Show that you understand the water cycle. Do at least one of the following:

- ☐ Explain why the planet's water is never used up.
- ☐ Trace the life of a raindrop.
- ☐ Show how a plant or animal takes in and gives off water.

☐ Purify water using a solar still.

☐ Figure out how a dinosaur's breath could recycle as a snowflake today.

9 Do one activity about the food chain in the sea or in fresh water.

☐ Trail a plankton net through the water and look closely at what you collect. Find out where plankton fits in a food chain you're part of. Imagine how much plankton it takes to feed a whale.

☐ Catch, dig, or buy food from the sea or fresh water. Clean and make a tasty dish with fish, shellfish, seaweed, watercress, or other such delicacies.

☐ Set up and keep up an aquarium for at least one week. Balance the numbers and kinds of living things with a healthy food and water supply.

10 Change the temperature of water to show how it acts in its three states: frozen, liquid, and gas. Show how you can get water to: float, push, become invisible, flow uphill, and form a cloud.

11 Figure out ways that water, wind, and weather go together. Tell when it's likely that one of the following will happen:

☐ a good breeze will come up for sailing, kite-flying, or other fun with wind on or near the water

☐ dew, frost, fog, or a cloud will form—and go away

☐ waves will build up and make it unsafe to go swimming or boating

☐ water will feel warmer than air that's the same temperature

12 Find out about working in the world of water in one of the following ways:

☐ Visit a place where water has been put to work, such as at a sewage or water treatment plant, an irrigation control center, a mining operation, a power plant, a fish hatchery, or a physical therapy center. Show that you know where the water comes from, how it works in the place you visit, where it goes, and what it's like at the end of the process.

☐ Tour a work boat, such as a ferry, barge, research vessel, tugboat, cargo ship, commercial fishing boat, dive boat, Navy vessel, or Coast Guard cutter. Ask people on board to compare their jobs on the water with similar jobs on land.

☐ Find out what it means to be an oceanographer, an hydrologist, or a limnologist. Look for ways that these jobs are like any other scientist's job and ways that the water setting makes them special.

My signature

Leader's signature   Date badge completed

The World of
the Arts

Dabbler

Complete one activity in each group.

A.1 Create a model of a building in which you would like to live, study, work, or play. Use inexpensive and/or scrap materials to create your model.

2 Decide what works of art help make a community more beautiful, such as fountains, statues, or murals. Choose one type and draw an original design that you feel would look good in your community.

B.1 Create a work of your own design that is intended to hang on a wall. This could be a painting, drawing, print, weaving, stitchery, macrame, or mixed media project. Display your piece at a troop or patrol meeting.

2 Create a work of your own design that is meant to be seen from all sides. This could be a sculpture, a piece of pottery, a mobile, or other design. Use clay, wood, plaster, plastic, metal, paper, or fibers. Display your piece at a troop or patrol meeting.

C.1 Learn about two different kinds of instruments from the four families (string, percussion, wind, and brass); how they sound, where and when they are played, etc. Make a simple instrument that you can use to accompany singing at your troop or patrol meeting.

2 Learn a new song and practice it with your friends until you know it well. If possible, tape your song and play it back to hear how you sound. Practice until you like the sound you hear. Then learn a round and sing it with your group.

D.1 Write a story or poem about something you know — yourself, your family, your favorite season of the year, your favorite holiday, a special place you like. Then write an imaginary story or poem. Share what you wrote with your troop or patrol.

2 Read a book. Then describe it to others in a newspaper review, a poster, or a play so that they will want to read it.

E.1 Design a room you would like — a playroom, a bedroom, a dining room, or a living room. Show your design in a painting, a drawing, or a diorama.

  2 Make an item for a home that would make it more beautiful. This could be a picture, a pillow, a wall hanging, or other decorative item.

F.1 Make plans to see a play, movie, or television drama as a troop or patrol. Afterwards, discuss with your group the kinds of things that made it interesting, dull, good, or bad. Take part in a dramatic skit, play, mime, musical, or dance performance either as a performer or as part of the backstage operation.

  2 See a puppet show either live, in the movies, or on television. Discuss the show and the puppets with your troop or patrol. Decide on a story, make your own puppets, and put on a show for your friends.

G.1 Design one of the following:
  ☐ a greeting card
  ☐ an advertisement to sell something
  ☐ a poster or leaflet
  ☐ a symbol or logo that would be your trademark

  2 Draw your own design for something new that would be useful — a car, a train, a plane, a can opener, a tool, a pot for cooking, a telephone, etc.

  Whichever activity you choose, share the results with your troop or patrol.

H.1 Find out about some of the folk art created in your area. If possible, talk to someone who knows about an art that was popular many years ago — quilting, wood carving, scrimshaw, toy making, egg decorating, lace making, embroidery, etc. Ask them to explain it to you and show you how it is done. Demonstrate what you have discovered to your troop or patrol.

  2 Choose a holiday that is celebrated by someone in your community or another country. Find out how this holiday is celebrated. Learn about and demonstrate any special songs, games, decorations, clothing, or other art forms that go with this holiday.

I.1 Design and make something for someone as a gift. Keep in mind the person's interests, likes, and dislikes. It could be a special box for a collection, a piece of jewelry or clothing, a plant holder, a toy, or a game. Show your design to your troop or patrol and explain why you made it for the person.

2 Look through a catalog, newspaper, or magazine and choose several articles of clothing for girls your age for different occasions. Cut them out or draw them and make posters of clothing that is comfortable and attractive for different kinds of weather or different occasions: for example, sunny, cold, or snowy days; parties, troop meetings, camping, school, religious services, traveling, sports, etc. Explain why you chose each outfit for each occasion.

J.1 Attend or watch a performance on television of a type of dance you have not seen before. Afterward, learn as much as you can about that dance form and present it to your troop in some manner.

2 Perform or participate in a dance recital, an ethnic dance festival, or a neighborhood, troop, or council folk or square dance.

My signature

Leader's signature   Date badge completed

Architecture

Complete five activities, including the two starred.

*1 Plan and take a walk in your community (or a city, town, or village you are visiting) to find examples of beauty in man-made objects, such as buildings, statues, fountains, and fences. Make a list. Also identify the objects or areas that are unattractive. Tell why you feel some are beautiful and some are not. Compare notes with others. Check those you think are works of art. Take photographs or make drawings of several of the items checked. Prepare a map to show someone else the route of your work and where your selected works of art are located.

2 Design a school that you would like to attend. Before you plan your school, ask yourself some of these questions:

☐ Would it be a plastic bubble floating on a lake, an outdoor school in the woods with a zoo in the middle, a skyscraper school?

☐ How would you enter your school — by a bridge, a rope, a tunnel, etc.?

☐ What kind of rooms and areas would your school have — garden, music and art rooms, lunchrooms, many small classrooms, or a few large work areas?

Consider how to save energy and how your school will fit in with other buildings around it. Draw it to scale on graph paper or make a model of your school with simple, inexpensive materials.

OR Design a house of the future. Decide where it will be — floating in space, on a planet, at a space station, under the ocean, etc. Draw the house to scale on graph paper or create a model of it and a plan for the transportation to get to it.

For either activity, show your scale drawing or model to others and explain why you designed it the way you did.

To make your own graph paper, draw lines on a sheet of paper at even intervals, for example, ½ inch apart.

3 Design a garden — perhaps a kids-only garden, a medieval garden, a storybook garden, or a garden that might be in another country. Make a space plan for your garden. Think about what will go into your garden — kinds of flowers and/or trees, sculptures, walkways, waterfalls or fountains, places to sit. Plan the entrance and center of your garden. When plans are complete, draw it to scale on graph paper or make a model of the garden using inexpensive materials.

OR Together with three or four other girls in the troop, design a neighborhood zoo. First, decide what animals will live in your zoo. Cut out or draw pictures of the animals. Find out what each animal eats and what else it needs to keep happy and healthy. Plan spaces for the animals, buildings, walls, pathways, plantings, water, and fun places for animals and how visitors will see the animals. With your team, make a model and give your zoo a name.

Whichever activity you choose, show your model to others and explain your plans.

To make your own graph paper, draw lines on a sheet of paper at even intervals, for example, ½ inch apart.

4 Show that you have learned about architecture throughout the world by creating a game, poster, exhibit, or mural which shows buildings in other parts of the country or other parts of the world. Include examples of four of the following types of buildings:
- ☐ one where there is a season with heavy rain and some dry spells
- ☐ one where there is cold weather most of the year with many forests
- ☐ one where there is cold weather with few trees
- ☐ one built on a river or other waterway
- ☐ one where people need protection from wild animals
- ☐ one where there are many mountains
- ☐ one where the weather is hot and dry all year
- ☐ one built for the religion of the people
- ☐ one that is unique and different from any you have seen

Prepare to explain to other people where the buildings are located and why they are built the way they are.

5 Create a plan for your community based on your list from activity number 1. Include things other than buildings that would make your community more beautiful as well as a better place to live, work, and play. Make certain the space you design can be used by people with disabilities. Make a drawing or model of your plan and explain why it would be appropriate.

6 Find out in what ways the following careers contribute to the beauty of buildings, parks, and towns: architect, landscape architect, sculptor, designer, urban planner. Arrange to interview at least one person in one of these careers. Ask about such things as: how the person decided on the career, what training or education is required, what kind of work is involved, what materials and tools are needed, how laws and building codes make a difference in designs. Present your findings to your troop or patrol in an interesting way.

7 Create an exhibit of pictures or actual samples of building materials and a drawing or picture of a building made from these materials. Explain why the material is right for each building shown.

8 Learn how to create floor plans to scale. Measure a room and the furnishings in it. Draw the room and the furniture to scale on graph paper, indicate the scale (for example, 1 inch = 1 foot) and display your scale drawing at a troop or patrol meeting.

To make your own graph paper, draw lines on a sheet of paper at even intervals, for example, ½ inch apart.

Do this last:

*9 Using what you have learned in other activities, plan, design, and construct with actual building materials and supplies a small structure, such as a dollhouse, bird feeder, or pet house.

My signature

Leader's signature   Date badge completed

Art
in the
Home

Complete six activities, including the one starred.

*1 Make a collection of pictures of different rooms showing different styles of furniture, rugs, wall coverings, decoration, lighting, and colors. Pictures can come from newspapers, magazines, or catalogs. Using your collection, do two of the following:

☐ Look over the different furniture styles and decide which you like best and why.

☐ Look at the patterns in the rooms in the pictures. How many patterns are there — on the floor, walls, windows, furniture? How do they go with each other? What mixture of pattern and plain color do you like best?

☐ Look at the colors and how they are used. Do different colors give different feelings? How are colors used together? Decide which three color combinations you like.

☐ Look at the lighting arrangements. How many different lighting fixtures can you find? What light is best for different activities in the home — reading, dining, cooking, sewing, etc.?

☐ Look at the decorations in the rooms in your pictures. Are there pictures, wall hangings, baskets, ceramics, collections, plants? Decide which type you like best and why.

2 Measure a room in a house. Draw it on a large piece of paper in scale, 1 inch = 1 foot. Indicate doors and windows. With paper of another color, cut shapes to scale for furniture, rugs, storage units, etc. Place these on the room drawing, in different arrangements that fit the size, shape, and purpose of the room. When satisfied, glue the shapes in place.

3 Find a large box. Collect samples of wallpaper, rugs, fabric, and paint colors. With your group or patrol, using the box as an experimental room, decide which wallpaper, rug, fabric, and color combinations each of you likes best. Then look through magazines and cut out pictures of the kind of furniture that would look good in your room. Plan how you would arrange the space of the room and what the room would be used for.

OR Using a cardboard or wooden box, create a dollhouse room, complete with rugs, wall covering, window treatment, and cardboard or wooden furniture.

4 Visit a store that sells plants and flowers. Study your pictures again to see how flowers and plants help decorate a room, or add plants or flowers to a box room you make. Create a floral arrangement or an arrangement of fruit or natural materials for a home or a party or pot a plant to give as a gift.

5 Create something using skills you already know or can learn from someone you know, that would beautify your home or someone else's home. Examples could be a basket, bookbinding, placemats, napkins or tablecloth, pillow, wall hanging, picture, baby's quilt, etc.

6 Visit a paint, hardware, or home decorating store. Study the types of paints, colors, finishes for wood, wallpapers, and the tools for applying these materials. Do one or more of the following:
- ☐ Paint a small piece of furniture.
- ☐ Finish or refinish a wood object or piece of furniture.
- ☐ Wallpaper something large enough so you can gain an understanding of the technique (a box, the inside of a bookcase, etc.) or help someone wallpaper or paint a room.

7 Find out something about the influences of other countries on furniture design or interior decoration. Collect magazine or newspaper pictures of three rooms containing furniture, rugs, or wall hangings that show the influence of another country. Be able to identify the country.

OR Find out how people from a culture other than yours decorate their homes for one of their holidays. Make or demonstrate how to make one decoration or craft you have learned.

8 Visit a store that sells furniture, rugs, china, table linens, curtains, and other household items or look through mail order catalogs. Select items that you think you would like in your home someday. List them and find out the price. Then make two plans for a room for your use, including the essentials you need for sleeping, storage, relaxing, homework, hobbies, etc. Make one plan if you had an unlimited budget, the other plan if you had very little money to spend.

9   Visit model homes or apartments, dollhouse exhibits, restoration or historical homes, friends' homes, model rooms in stores or museums, or take a house and garden tour or go to an open house. Make notes or sketches of the things you like — the furniture, decorations, rugs, quilts, windows, china, paintings. After you return, do a painting from memory of your favorite room. Be able to explain to your group why you made your choices.

10 Design and make or assemble a creative arrangement for storage, a place to keep your things, a way to provide space for a hobby, or a way to display a collection.

My signature

Leader's signature   Date badge completed

Art
in the
Round

Complete two activities from section A,
three from one category of section B, and two from section C.

A.1 Create an imaginary figure out of available materials, such as cardboard boxes or rolls, glue, string, paint, and assorted bits of scrap material. .

2 Create a structure that is pleasing to you out of twigs, small pieces of driftwood, toothpicks, coffee stirrer sticks, or a combination of such small sticks. Use glue, string, and tools appropriate to the materials.

3 Create a three-dimensional design in wire, by twisting, cutting, and/or coiling. Use tools appropriate to the heaviness of the wire and your design. Add other materials as needed for your design. Use as a stabile or a mobile.

4 With a lump of clay, demonstrate the difference between modeling and carving.

5 From a plaster block, create a three-dimensional figure, or a bas-relief. Be able to demonstrate or explain how plaster is mixed and poured into the mold.

6 Create an abstract piece of sculpture using boxes, crates, pieces of wood, cardboard, or polystyrene. Include negative as well as positive space in your design.

7 Make a pinch pot in clay and decorate it with slip decoration, or sgraffito.

B Choose one of the categories in section B and do three activities in that group. After completing the activities, display or exhibit your accomplishments at a troop, patrol, or other Girl Scout gathering.

1 Clay
   - [ ] Learn about various types of clay and glazes, know how an unfinished piece of pottery is kept damp and how it is cared for between working periods.
   - [ ] Help build a simple outdoor kiln for troop, camp, school, or community use.
   - [ ] Learn how a kiln is stacked, and if possible, help stack one.
   - [ ] Make a piece of pottery, using the coil method, and finish it with a glaze.
   - [ ] Make a tile or pottery piece (box, etc.), using the slab method. Apply a design in slip, sgraffito, incising carving, or painted design. If possible, glaze and fire it.
   - [ ] Make a figure or form in clay. If possible, glaze and have it fired. Be able to explain the difference between ceramics and pottery.

2 Paper
   - [ ] Create a papier-mâché mask to be worn as part of a play or festival or to be used as decoration.
   - [ ] Create a sculpture in papier-mâché over wire, boxes, or other forms.
   - [ ] Create a decoration for a party or holiday from cardboard or paper.
   - [ ] Create a useful object from papier-mâché.
   - [ ] Using stiff paper, create sculpture-like designs by cutting, folding, coiling, rolling, glueing, and taping.

3 Wood, Plaster, and Sculpture Material
   - [ ] Carve a sculpture in soft wood. Finish it and be able to explain the tools and equipment used in wood carving.
   - [ ] Mix plaster of paris to be sculpture material. Pour into a mold. When the mold is ready, carve a design in the round.
   - [ ] Create a relief design in plaster and sand using natural materials as part of your design.
   - [ ] Find out about three different kinds of wood that can be used for carving, and experiment with carving them. Be able to explain which ones you feel are best and why.
   - [ ] Create a sculpture in a sculpture material other than wood or plaster.

C.1 Visit a museum, gallery, studio, art show, crafts fair, sales shop, or other place where sculpture in various materials and different kinds of pottery and ceramics are on display. Be ready to explain what you liked best and why.

2 Visit a studio where you can observe a sculptor at work, a commercial pottery, or a professional potter's studio. Ask questions about the kind of work being done, and also about the way the people became involved in this career and the kinds of training they received.

3 Collect pictures and read about some outstanding pieces of sculpture in the United States or another country; know about the artist and the kind of work she/he did or does.

OR Collect pictures of pottery or ceramics, read about these works or the artists who created them and be able to explain something about the items and why you selected them.

4 Know the meaning of "in-the-round" and "in-relief." Find examples of these in your community and draw or photograph them.

OR Find pictures or examples of pottery that is used today. Select some you feel are beautiful for the purpose designed and be able to tell something about the different kinds of pottery in use today.

5 Find examples of folk sculpture or folk pottery. Look for pictures in magazines and books, or sketch what you see in museums or exhibits. Choose three different examples to display at troop or patrol meetings or other Girl Scout gathering. These examples can be from three countries outside the United States, three sections of the United States, or a combination. Label each with where it is found and the material used.

My signature

Leader's signature   Date badge completed

Art to Wear

Complete four activities.
Do at least one activity from each section,
including the one starred in section A.

A.1 Design an outfit for yourself or for someone else that you think is right for you or that person. Choose an outfit for school, camping, sports, or a party. List or show colors and fabrics on your sketch.

2 Find three different types of fashion illustrations in magazines and/or newspapers. With the help of an art teacher or other adult, make fashion sketches of three outfits.

*3 Learn to sew a simple garment for yourself or someone else, using a pattern and sewing machine, if possible. If necessary, ask an adult to help you learn.

4 Create a poster of traditional dress of countries from three continents. Explore libraries, museums, magazines, or talk to family and friends to find out how the garments or decorations reflect the culture and lifestyle of the people.

5 Find pictures of fashions from four periods of history, approximately 20 years apart (example: 1750, 1770, 1790, 1810 or 1900, 1920, 1940, 1960). List the similarities, differences, and any trends that show up in different periods.

B.1 Find out about the kinds of decoration that may be added to clothing to beautify or make it more personal. Learn one of the following and create a small decorative item for yourself or someone else.

- [ ] embroidery or crewel
- [ ] crocheting or knitting
- [ ] finger or other belt weaving
- [ ] macrame
- [ ] lacework or tatting
- [ ] quilting
- [ ] appliqué
- [ ] braiding of yarn, threads, or ribbon
- [ ] wrapping (using yarn over a cord)
- [ ] tassels, fringe, pompoms

Add other decorative touches if you wish, such as beads, natural materials, or buttons.

2 Fabric and fashion go together. Weave a small square of fabric on a simple loom. Make a poster, display cards, or booklet showing eight different fabrics. Label each fabric and give some information about it. Choose from these:

☐ weaves, such as twill, tabby, tapestry, brocade, pile
☐ knitted
☐ nonwoven
☐ gauze
☐ natural fibers
☐ manufactured fibers
☐ combinations of natural and manufactured fibers
☐ printed and woven designs
☐ water repellent or other finish

3 Designs or patterns are created in fabrics by means other than weaving—batik, stencil, tie-dye, silk screen are a few of these. Select one method and create a simple design or an allover pattern. Use it on a shirt, or other clothing, or a plain piece of fabric.

4 Look in stores, magazines, newspapers, craft shows, and fairs to find examples of jewelry and ornaments that have been handmade or could be handmade. Make a list of techniques, such as work in metal, clay, beads, natural materials, crochet, warp wrapping, knotting, weaving; learn one and create your own piece of jewelry or hair ornament.

C.1 Find out what looks best on you. With your patrol or friends, make full-size silhouettes of each other by drawing around the outlines of your body. Cut from plain paper different shapes of dresses, skirts, pants, jackets, blouses, and place them against each silhouette. Decide which looks best on each silhouette.

OR Measure your own face, then draw your face in actual size on a piece of paper. Make several different styles of hair out of heavy paper and try them fitted around the drawing of your face. Decide which ones look best on you.

OR In front of a mirror, place several large pieces of colored paper or fabric under your chin and around your face. Decide which colors are best for your skin, hair, and eyes.

2 Create a clothing accessory for yourself, such as a jacket, a vest, a belt, a scarf, or a hat, in a technique that you have learned: sewing, knitting, crocheting, embroidering.

My signature

Leader's signature   Date badge completed

Books

Complete six activities.

1   Explore your local library's resources. Prepare a brochure about the library for new residents, a poster to encourage greater use of the library or an advertising flyer to let the community know what the library has to offer. Be sure to include information on the kinds of books, tapes and records, exhibits and special programs, newspapers, magazines, and audiovisuals available for children and adults. Find out what help is available and what you can borrow from the library besides books.

2   Find out about the folktales, stories, poems, plays, and/or writers in a culture other than your own. You may find out this information by talking to someone from that culture, by searching in the library, or by watching a special television show. Share what you have learned by acting out one or more of the stories or folktales; telling about one or more of the writers of that culture; reading one of the stories, poems, or folktales to your Girl Scout group or another audience; or by creating puppets for one of the tales and putting on a puppet show for a group.

3   Read a book especially for this badge. After reading, tell members of your troop or other group about the book.

OR   Write up an annotated list of at least ten books you believe a girl your age would like to read. (An annotated list includes title, author, publisher, and a short description of each book.) Include different kinds of books in your list. Be sure you have read them.

4   Write one of the following:
☐ an original short story of at least 100 words
☐ a different ending to a story or play you already know

5 Design a set of book covers for three books or stories.

OR Create illustrations for a familiar story, folktale, or poem.

OR Ask your school or community librarian to show you books illustrated by five children's artists, particularly Caldecott Medal winners. Borrow the books and make a troop display, if possible.

OR Look at illustrations of three or more nursery rhymes or ABC books to see which ones you think a little child would enjoy. Create your own illustrated ABC book for a child.

6 Collect books, paperbacks, and magazines appropriate for one age level. Give them to a library at a camp, nursing home, youth shelter, well baby clinic, day-care center, or veterans' hospital.

OR Select books, magazine articles, jokes, riddles, poetry, or short stories and make a tape of some selections to give to someone who may not be able to read at the present time.

OR Set up a schedule with other troop members to bring books from your local library in large print, braille, or on tape to someone who would enjoy them.

OR Volunteer to work at your local library.

OR As a troop project, collect books that are appropriate for children and young people and set up a lending library for your own troop or for several troops in your area. Work out a plan for girls to take turns being librarian. Volunteer to help someone learn to read better.

7 Find out about careers with books. You might visit with an author, poet, illustrator, editor, or someone who publishes books. Draw a diagram of how a book gets from the idea stage to the printed page. Visit a publishing house, if possible.

8 Read a variety of stories, poems, or folktales that give you an idea of the literature of the United States. What do these stories tell you about the way people lived, what kind of houses they lived in, what they wore, what they ate, etc.? Draw a large map of the United States and place drawings, authors, and books in various parts of the country or make a diorama of one example that you read.

9 Read a long poem and a short poem that you like. Then do one of these activities:
   ☐ Find a piece of artwork, do a floral arrangement, or select a piece of music that would go with one of the poems.
   ☐ Read several other poems by the same poet.
   ☐ Write your own poetry and identify the form you are using: limerick, jingle, haiku, narrative, etc.

10 Find out from your local librarian or school librarian a list of Newbery Award-winning books. If you have not read any of these books, read at least one. Then, make a decorative bookmark, book poster, or promotional flyer about Newbery books.

OR In a newspaper or other source from your community, read reviews of new books for your age level. Check one of these books out of the library, read, and review it yourself. Was your review the same as or different from the review you read?

11 Learn how to mend books and do a simple bookbinding. Mend a favorite paperback book or do a bookbinding for your original writing accomplished for this badge.

My signature

Leader's signature   Date badge completed

Communication Arts

Complete two activities from section A, two from section B, one from section C, and one from section D.

A Communications — Verbal

1 Write a story or poem that communicates an idea you want to get across. Read it to a group. Did they get your message? If not, how could you change the story or poem so that they do get your message?

2 Choose a story or poem that you feel tells very well what the artist wanted to say. Read your selection to a group.

3 Look at headlines in newspapers and magazines. Make up some headlines for events, such as the arrival of the first tourists on Mars, the end of all wars and fighting in the world, a spectacular achievement of a ten-year-old girl.

4 Write a short news story about an event in your school or troop. Submit it to the school newspaper or council bulletin.

5 Participate in a debate, or prepare and give a two-minute speech on a favorite subject.

6 Read a play to discover how plays communicate differently from stories or poems. Write a short play, puppet show, Scouts' Own, radio show, or other dramatic performance.

7 Write a plan for a publicity campaign for a candidate of your choice in a make-believe election or write a radio advertisement for a new product to show how words communicate in selling or advertising.

B Communications — Visual

1 With a still or movie camera, take pictures of two of these: a windstorm or other happening in nature; pollution or other environmental concern; something that expresses quiet beauty, joy, or excitement.

2 Take photographs or sketch scenes which tell a story without the need for words. Each photograph or sketch may tell a small story on its own or several can be put together to form a story.

3 Take photographs that can be used to advertise something. Try at least two of the ones listed below. Do several views of each and

decide on one that you think will most likely sell the item.

- ☐ a house, farm, store, or business for sale
- ☐ new or used carpentry, plumbing, or kitchen tools
- ☐ a spot to visit or a site to see
- ☐ a used car, bicycle, motorcycle, trailer, camper, or motorbike
- ☐ a handmade item
- ☐ shoes, boots, sneakers, moccasins, or sandals

4 Do a painting, print, pen and ink drawing, or other visual art that communicates a feeling or an idea. Display it to your patrol or other group and see if they can tell what the message is.

5 Make a list of a variety of commercial visual designs you see in a week. Include such things as billboards, posters, signs, packages, etc. Look at them to see how they use color, lettering, and space; decide which are best. Choose a theme and make a poster that catches the eye and gives a message without many words.

6 Put together a collage or poster with examples of pictures of a variety of communications, such as semaphore, braille, sign language, signal flags, international road signs, distress signals, referee's signals. Learn one set of the above examples and teach someone else.

7 Collect examples or draw familiar symbols and logos that immediately convey a message. Arrange these in poster form. Design a logo for: yourself, to print on your stationery, book covers, etc.; your troop as an identifying symbol; or a special event that is happening in your school or Girl Scout council.

C **Communications — Visual and Verbal**

Many times visual images combine with words (spoken or written) to create a communication using both forms.

1 Attend a live theater production, an opera, or a musical. Afterwards, write up a short review as a newspaper reviewer would do, telling how the visual and the verbal worked together to communicate something to the audience.

2 After looking through several magazines, put together your own magazine of at least 16 pages showing how magazines use words and pictures together.

3 Look through several books that combine visuals with words. Decide which books really must have both visuals and words, which ones might have used only one or the other. Create one of the following: a travel book, an art book, or a child's beginning reader.

4 Movies, television, and slide shows also use words and pictures. Tell how your favorite movie, television show, or slide show combines words and visuals to get across the message. Do a storyboard (a plan showing a drawing of each picture and words that go with it) for a two-minute movie, television short, or slide show that shows how you would use pictures and words together.

D Some other ways to communicate

1 If possible, visit a radio or television station. Visit the studios and find out how a show is produced. Listen to several radio shows. Create the script, sound effects, and format for a news program, a disc jockey program, an interview talk show, or a program you select.

OR Investigate ham radio and how it works. Learn how to get a license. If possible, see a ham radio in operation. Prepare a short broadcast for a ham radio operator to report and seek help in a disaster. Use Morse code.

2 After doing other requirements for this badge, prepare a list of careers in communications, based on your activities. Pick out one and explain why you might want to pursue it.

OR Do an activity from **Careers to Explore for Brownie and Junior Girl Scouts** that relates to communications careers.

3 Attend a performance of music or dance and analyze how these art forms communicate. Prepare a musical (records) program to put on for others that is based on a theme.

OR With your patrol or group, prepare a dance program that communicates a story or theme and put it on for some people.

4 Find out the languages that are spoken in your community and learn enough phrases in one of those languages to be able to carry on a short conversation.

5 Show that you have discovered the kinds of communications needed in public relations promotional work by outlining what you would plan for one of the following:

☐ a party at the opening of an art exhibit to introduce a new artist to the community

☐ a tour of your local area to encourage business people to set up shops in the area

☐ a workshop to acquaint the parents and children with the new facilities at the science center

☐ a ceremony for an awards presentation for your troop

☐ a conference for international visitors, to acquaint them with your community

My signature

Leader's signature   Date badge completed

Dance

Complete six activities, including the one starred.

1 Select a piece of music and move your body to this music, using at least half of these suggested movements: swing, bend, turn, stretch, pull, push, twist, strike, dodge, shake, bounce, hop, skip, walk, gallop, jump, or run.

2 Demonstrate in body movements at least two of the following:
- [ ] the feelings that a particular piece of music brings out in you
- [ ] the ways people move (athletes, waiters, young people, old people, conductors, cooks, traffic directors, etc.)
- [ ] an expression of nature, such as trees moving in the wind; a story; movements of machines; a dramatic situation, such as missing a train, saying goodbye to someone, or meeting old friends.

Then make up a dance by yourself, with a partner, or with a group, using movements from one of the areas you selected.

3 Attend a dance concert or a dance class. Make an appointment first, and after the concert, talk to the performers or the teachers about their work, using questions you prepared before going.

OR Go to a movie musical (or watch one on television) and discuss the dancing sequences with your patrol or friends. Be prepared to describe how the dancing adds to the production. Find out the name of the choreographer; learn something about this person's career and work.

*4 Participate in a dance program either as a soloist or as part of a group. Share your experience with others.

5 Learn about three different types of social dancing and demonstrate to your patrol or group how to do them. Consider the polka, waltz, tango, fox trot, lindy, Charleston, jitterbug, jazz, disco, or current dance steps.

6 Explore the dance of three countries other than your own. Choose at least one other continent. Investigate what the dance means in that culture, and something about the costumes, seasons, or festivities that might be associated with it. Demonstrate what you find out.

7 Explore the dance of the United States in three different areas of the country and two different periods of time. Create costumes appropriate for these and put on a demonstration to teach others.

8 Listen to several recordings of dance music — folk, ethnic, theater, ballet, or music hall. Using steps you know, create a new dance to go with at least two types of music. You may want to use percussion instruments, such as tambourines or drums, with one dance.

9 With your troop or patrol, hold a party or social gathering which includes dancing. You may teach a new dance, use a traditional dance form, or plan well-known dances. Try to include most of the guests in the dancing.

My signature

Leader's signature

Date badge completed

Folk Arts

Complete six activities.

1. Draw or paint a picture of yourself or of your whole family, as it might have been done by a folk artist before cameras were invented. Put some things in the background that are very special about you or your family.

OR Look at some old photographs of your family or groups of people. Compare them with some recent ones of yourself, your friends, or of other people. Are there differences in the poses, the clothes, the expressions? What kinds of feelings do you get about the people in the pictures? Write a short story about what the pictures tell you.

OR Tell a story about yourself in a painting or picture. Share this with some friends.

2. Learn something about the tradition of storytelling. If possible, get together with someone who is a good storyteller and learn some of the special ways to make your audience want to keep listening. Read a fairy tale, myth, or legend that you like and be able to tell it to a group, perhaps as part of a ceremony or special event.

3. Choose a section of our country and find out about the folk toys made there long ago and today. Make a folk toy or game and plan to share it with a special child or friend.

OR Find out about puppets from several countries. Design and make a puppet. Plan a puppet show and have your puppet act out a folktale or legend or your own play.

4. Learn a folk dance from your part of the country or one from a country that interests you. Teach it to some friends. Put together a simple costume or part of a costume and find an opportunity to perform your dance for someone else.

OR Learn a folk song or ballad that tells a story about people, places, or events. Be able to explain the story behind the song and teach the words to your friends or patrol. Work out actions if you like and perform for someone.

5 Ask someone to teach you or find directions for making a whistle, drum, or other folk instrument. Make one and demonstrate its use to your troop or friends.

OR Study about folk instruments and the people who made them. Be able to tell something about the traditional ways these people have used the instruments. Show pictures or drawings of the instruments when you explain them to your group.

6 Look for examples and pictures of traditional folk arts from at least three countries. Try a project for which you can find the instructions or someone to teach you. Some ideas might be: quilling, origami, pysanky eggs, pinatas, ceremonial masks, jewelry, traditional foods, and ceremonies.

7 If you feel you have gotten into the swing of a particular folk art, plan a gathering during which you will teach others, have fun together, and perhaps all work on a large project that would be difficult without lots of helping hands. Some examples might be: a quilting bee, a cornhusking party, a taffy pull, a kite festival.

OR Create your own new folk art project based on the spirit of some you have learned about while doing this badge.

8 Find directions and recipes for some of the following:
- [ ] drying fruits
- [ ] herb teas
- [ ] traditional sourdough or herb breads
- [ ] natural food cooking
- [ ] apple dolls
- [ ] dried flower arrangements
- [ ] holiday decorations
- [ ] wok cooking

Perhaps an older friend or adult might enjoy working with you. Try at least one project.

9 Many useful and decorative things that are now machine-made and easily found in stores were once all handmade using natural materials and handcraft processes. Some examples are pottery, baskets, woodwork, candles, soap, paper, threads, and dyes for yarns and cloth. Add other things you can think of to this list and think about the materials it would take to do each. Are they available? Would using them be harmful to the environment? Would making some of these involve some special health and safety procedures?

Find examples or pictures of some of these folk arts that interest you. Then, ask your leader, an adult friend, or a person from your community to help you learn how to do one craft using natural materials.

10 Make a list of some of the things a girl your age would have been learning to do 200 years ago in America to accomplish the necessities of life (for example, clothing, food, shelter, utensils, etc.). Did men and women have certain jobs that were expected of them? Is this different now?

OR Find some articles belonging to your family, that have been passed down from person to person. Share these in some way with your friends or troop, explaining what they are and where they came from.

OR Visit a place near you where antiques, personal belongings of people who lived in past years, or collections of folk arts are on display. You might find these at restorations, museums, or places designated as historic landmarks. Find out what makes them special and what life was like when they originated.

My signature

Leader's signature   Date badge completed

Musician

Complete five activities, including the one starred.

1 Writing music is an art that requires much skill and training, but you can start in fairly simple ways.

If you play an instrument, write a simple melody for that instrument of at least eight measures. Notate your piece using symbols for key, tempo, and dynamics and teach it to someone else.

OR Make up words and music for a nonsense song about something funny that happened in your troop or at camp.

OR Do a jazz improvisation of a popular song.

2 Finding out about the background of a piece of music helps us appreciate the music today. Do one of the following:

☐ Find out about the life and works of a living composer or performer. Using tapes or records, give a 30-minute program to tell others about the musician.

☐ Learn about early singing groups — minstrels, troubadours, minnesingers, and meistersingers. Sing at least one song from this period, and explain about the group, the time, and the country where it was found.

☐ Listen to a musical composition that tells a story. Find out all you can about the music and the composer; then try to sell the record to your leader or another adult by a simulated television commercial or movie advertisement.

3 Listen to and watch an opera or operetta live or on television. Listen for the story idea, how much is sung, or spoken, what language it is in, how the voices are related to the characters, who the composer was, and when she/he lived. Be able to tell the story of the opera or operetta to a group. Illustrate your talk in some manner.

OR Learn to sing a ballad. Dramatize it or make a shadowgraph or puppet show of it.

OR Listen to and see a ballet or concert, live or on television. Choose several other pieces of music that you feel would be appropriate as dances and create a dance for one of them.

4 Participate in a musical performance using your musical skills in at least one of the following: music for a Scouts' Own, an individual

instrument or voice recital, a group performance, a musical extravaganza, or a neighborhood or community musical event.

*5 Expand your knowledge of songs by learning at least three new songs well enough to perform them. Include two-part or three-part songs, songs with descants, songs in languages other than your own. Be able to tell something about your songs and tell what the meaning is, if a song is in another language.

6 Share your musical knowledge.

Learn three action songs suitable for young children. Teach them to Brownie Girl Scouts or to a school or church group.

OR Teach young children how to make simple rhythm instruments and play them.

OR Do a poster for a Girl Scout or other group to show the arrangements of instruments in an orchestra. Identify the instruments and the section to which they belong.

OR Make a bulletin board display or exhibit depicting a famous composer, an era in musical history, or the history of your instrument.

OR Have a musical sharing afternoon or evening with a senior citizens' group, where you and other people share favorite songs or instrumental favorites.

7 Program music is orchestral music with a theme or story. Pretend that you are selecting the music for a concert for people who like three of the things listed below. Give the name of the music and the composer, and possibly a recording of your selection.
☐ the sea or rivers   ☐ patriotism, parades
☐ woods or mountains   ☐ elves, leprechauns, or fairies
☐ fields or meadows   ☐ religious feeling (other than hymn)
☐ circus or festival

8 Choose three pieces of music heard in concerts or on radio, television, or recordings that show the influence of a country outside the United States. These might include dance music from other countries, calypso or other rhythms, or songs in another language. Play or sing them for your troop or group and be able to explain what these influences are.

My signature

Leader's signature   Date badge completed

Music
Lover

Complete six activities, including the one starred.

1 Select a favorite piece of music and create a rhythmic accompaniment to go with it. Use a rhythm instrument you have made or select a variety of items that will give you the tone and sound you want. If possible, tape a performance of your piece with its accompaniment and see if others can guess the materials used for the sound.

2 Listen to several records and choose one you feel is suitable for dancing. Create a dance that you and a group can do in time with the music.

OR Learn two singing games and play them with your troop or teach them to others.

3 Listen to a piece of music and explain what the music says to you by doing one of the following.

Create a design or picture with paint.

OR Do an interpretation of the music in creative movement.

OR Create a poem that the music inspires.

*4 Learn three songs well enough to sing them to a group or teach others. Choose from among these types of songs: a round, a folk song used to accompany work, a song that expresses the religious life of people, a grace.

5 Learn folk songs from five different countries on three different continents. Learn as much as you can about these songs. Create an illustration that you feel might go with two of the songs in a songbook.

6 Interview a musician (or a music teacher). Find out why that person chose music as a career. Learn what preparation was necessary and what the person enjoys about her/his career. Write up a career interview with drawings to tell about that career.

7 Find three songs on records or in a music book that were popular music in another period of history and that tell something about that period. Choose a song of today and explain how it tells a story of today's times.

8 Have listening sessions, alone or with others, to listen to records or tapes, a concert on television or radio, or a live concert. Listen to at least two of the following: a symphony, musical comedy, opera or operetta, chamber music, jazz, popular or band music, and a variety of large or small orchestras, single instruments, voices, choruses. After you have done this, do one of the following:

☐ Write a note to a friend or relative telling about the session.

☐ Write an imaginary letter to the composer or musician telling two or three things you liked best.

☐ Give a brief demonstration by means of a record or tape about the kind of music you heard or something about the instruments. Explain the type of musical style and include any pictures that will help others understand the demonstration.

9 Participate in a performance as a soloist or as part of a group in a vocal or instrumental concert or performance. After the concert, share with others what you know about one of the pieces performed or something special about your instrument.

My signature

Leader's signature   Date badge completed

Popular Arts

Complete four activities.

1 Find seven examples of symbols, such as the American eagle. Draw some simple shapes that could be used for symbols of things familiar to you. Design your own coat of arms using symbols to depict yourself or your family. See if others can guess the meaning of your symbols.

OR Look for pictures of symbols or symbolic designs and find out all you can about the people for whom these symbols were or are important. Here are some things to look at: American Indian jewelry, colonial crewel work, African pottery, Norwegian rosemaling, Pennsylvania German hex signs and quilts, oriental brush painting, church windows, masks and headdresses, holiday ornaments, rugs, and tapestries. Create a poster that shows the symbols you have collected and where they originated.

2 Look around your home, school, stores, or community to see how many things you can find that have been decorated by hand. Find, through pictures or actual examples, several items, such as decorated tinware (tole painting), scrimshaw, painted furniture, painted wooden objects (boxes, etc.), decorated chinaware or pottery, stenciled walls and floors, decorative carvings for interior walls, windows, decorated textiles. Choose one to learn more about. Find someone to teach you, if you can, and create one work of art with your own decoration. Use some of your symbols in your design.

OR Visit a folk art museum or restoration where you can see examples of the folk arts listed above. Learn from booklets or demonstrations and create one art piece.

3 Learn about quilting terms and techniques. What are patchwork or pieced designs, appliqué, trapunto, tufting, embroidery, quilting? Learn how to cut out shapes for pieced designs and appliqué, and how to plan and transfer designs onto fabric for other processes. Do samples and diagrams so that you can teach others.

4 Make a sampler to demonstrate your skill in one of the following. Find someone to teach you the skill if you need help.
   - [ ] needlepoint
   - [ ] crewel
   - [ ] knitting
   - [ ] knotting (macrame)
   - [ ] cross-stitch
   - [ ] crochet

5 Look for examples of woven materials and pictures of looms from different areas of our country and other parts of the world, such as Africa, Mexico, the Orient, Scandinavia, and India. Notice the patterns and colors, and if you can, how they feel. What do the colors and designs tell you about the way of life of the people? How do the looms relate to the finished fabric? Create a small handmade loom and weave a small swatch on it.

OR Visit a place where you can see weaving and looms. Find out about simple looms you can make yourself. Learn about several types of weaving and the terms used to describe weaving. Here are some to start thinking about: warp and weft (or woof), tabby weave, pattern weaving, tapestry weaving, rya, shuttle, loom, heddles. Add others that you find. Get together with your patrol or badge group and find a way to make, or have someone help you make, a loom you can share and add to the troop equipment.

6 Learn tales and legends from three countries and create a puppet show, letter and illustrate a booklet, or conduct a storytelling hour for younger children.

7 Learn folk dances from three countries and write them down, find or tape music, and get a group of friends together and teach them the dances.

8 Draw or find pictures of five instruments that accompany folk music of another country. Be able to demonstrate or play recordings of some of these instruments or simulate the sound with your own instrument.

9 Learn five additional folk songs from five countries on three different continents and be able to explain something about them and what they mean in that culture.

My signature

Leader's signature   Date badge completed

Prints and Graphics

Complete two activities from section A, three from section B including the one starred, and one from section C.

A.1 Collect items, such as bottle caps, spools, screws, sponges, sticks, woodblocks, and tube caps with which to make impression or gadget prints. Use a stamp pad for printing. Experiment with one item at a time to create a border design, an allover design, and a design in two colors. Then try combinations of several items to make a print design.

  2 Experiment with at least two other kinds of prints, such as spatter prints, smoke prints, sun prints, blueprints, photograms. Make a finished print of one to use for some purpose.

  3 Experiment with at least two methods of printmaking, using materials, such as corrugated cardboard, rubber cement, wax or plaster of paris, styrofoam, or a new commercial printing material. Make a finished print to use for some purpose.

  4 Explore the printing processes as they apply to the printing of books. Find out about type and how it was used in the early days of the printing press. Find four different styles of typeface in magazines or newspapers. Compare them to see in what kinds of books, advertisements, or posters they would work best. Choose one you like best and design a page of a book including the typeface, an illustration (line drawing or photograph), and borders — or choose one and design three slides which might open a filmstrip or slide show giving title, credits, and some line design.

B.1 Make two transfer prints with leaves, fern, or bark.

  2 Make four rubbings of something raised or engraved, such as carved wood, a coin, a design on an iron gate, a gravestone, a leaf, a brick, a stone, a manhole cover, a rubber floor mat, etc.

  3 Make a relief print by cutting your design in an eraser, potato, turnip, or by glueing a felt, rubber, or cardboard design to heavy cardboard or a block of wood.

4 Create a design and cut a stencil for it. Show a safe way to use a stencil knife. Print your stenciled design on paper or fabric.

5 With a paper stencil on a simple silk screen, print your own design on paper or cloth.

6 Learn how to do a linoleum block print. Create the design; cut, and print one for a greeting card, bookplate, gift wrapping, or other project of your choice.

*7 Make a scrapbook of the different prints you have made, label each, and choose a suitable mat and frame for one of your prints to use in your home or give as a gift, or use one of your print designs as a wall hanging.

C.1 Visit an exhibit that includes several kinds of prints. Try to visit a printmaker and see her/him at work. Ask about the kind of work she/he does and why she/he chose this occupation.

2 Find out how stenciling was used by early settlers in this country. Be able to explain and illustrate at least two examples, such as Hitchcock or other stenciled furniture, wallpapers, floors, textiles, or toleware.

3 Use your printmaking skills to carry out a service project, such as making notepaper, cards, or bookplates for a church or other organization, programs or posters for some event, curtains for a day-care center, or some other project of your choice.

4 By searching through books, magazines, newspapers, museum prints, or art collections discover five different examples of how prints are used in countries outside the United States. Be able to explain the technique and something that makes the designs unique.

OR Collect pictures of five historical or contemporary printmakers— arrange an exhibit and give artist's name, period or dates, and technique used.

My signature

Leader's signature   Date badge completed

Textiles and Fibers

Complete four activities: one in section A,
two in one category of section B,
and one in section C.

There are many different kinds of textiles and arts using yarns, threads, and fibers.

A.1 Gather samples or pictures of five types of weaving, embroidery, crewelwork, needlepoint, hemstitching, or printed or batik dyed fabric. Make a display of your collection and label each example.

OR Learn about five distinctive types of textiles, weaving, and needle-work from other countries. Show samples or pictures and share your knowledge with your troop or friends.

2 Visit a museum, an historical restoration, or an exhibit and identify at least five types of needlework or textiles in clothes or household articles of previous years. Are they different from what we use today? How?

OR Attend a needlework or textiles show and/or demonstration. Talk to the people who do the weaving or needlework. Think about what you would like to make and what you need to learn before you make it.

3 Visit a textile mill and see how fabrics are processed. Discuss the differences between handmade and machine-made fabrics. Learn five different fibers from which textiles are made and be able to explain something about each.

Share your finished products with your troop or patrol.

B.1 Weaving—do at least two of the following:
- ☐ Weave something on a cardboard loom.
- ☐ Do a tapestry weaving on a cardboard or other type of loom.
- ☐ Make and thread a simple loom (such as a back-strap or flat frame). Demonstrate how to use it and weave something on it.
- ☐ On a simple loom, experiment with different textures, using various materials for warp and weft.
- ☐ Make a belt with finger weaving, tub weaving, or some other type of narrow weaving.
- ☐ Create a basket in a woven, coil, braided, or twining technique.

2 Knitting, crochet, or macrame — do at least two of the following:

- [ ] Demonstrate the following knots: overhand, square, half hitch, clove hitch, lark's head, sheepshank, bowline, taut line hitch, sheet bend, granny knot. Make a macrame sampler experimenting with colors, beads, textures, and several knots.
- [ ] Macrame a flat item, such as a place mat, doormat, wall hanging, etc.
- [ ] Do a simple macrame project, such as a belt or bookmark, using only a square knot; make the knots as even and precise as possible.
- [ ] Create your own macrame, knit, or crochet design for a gift, an item for your home, or for camp equipment.
- [ ] In knitting, learn to cast on, bind off, knit, purl, and yarn over. Select a suitable yarn and pattern and knit a small garment or accessory.
- [ ] In crochet, learn to start, finish, do chain, single crochet, double crochet, and afghan stitches. Select a suitable thread or yarn and pattern and crochet one small article.

3 Printed textiles—do at least two of the following:

- [ ] Create two simple border designs for a piece of fabric.
- [ ] Adapt one for a stencil, cut the stencil and, using one color, decorate some useful item.
- [ ] Cut a linoleum block and print a one-color design on some household item or garment.
- [ ] Design a paper cutting or paper folding and use it to create a repeat or allover pattern on fabric, a garment, or a household item.
- [ ] Learn about commercial dyes. Use one to dye or tint an article. Learn about textile paints.
- [ ] Make a tie-dyed article, using at least two kinds of tying but only one dye bath.

4 Hooking, braiding, or quilting—do at least two of the following:

- [ ] Learn something about hooked rugs and their history.
- [ ] Hook a small article, such as a chair seat or a pillow top.
- [ ] Learn something about making braided rugs from a variety of materials. Make a small braided piece for a chair, a bench, or a footstool.
- [ ] Gather several pictures or samples of quilts, including pieced, embroidered, appliquéd, and ornamental quilting.
- [ ] Make a quilt square of any type.
- [ ] Find out about different types of quilts. Compare old and new quilts. Make a small quilted article.

5 Embroidery and needlepoint—do at least two of the following:

☐ Learn to do eight of the following stitches and do a sampler to display your accomplishments: outline stitch, chain stitch, cross-stitch, back stitch, blanket stitch, satin stitch, darning stitch, French knot, lazy daisy, couching.

☐ Using five stitches you know, create your own picture or wall hanging, or decorate a garment or a household article.

☐ Work out a design on graph paper for counted thread work. Use the design to make a small piece of needlepoint or cross-stitch.

☐ Convert a design or your initials to graph paper and show four ways that graph designs can be used (such as cross-stitch, needlepoint, beading, or knitting). Choose one way to make a small sample of your design.

C.1 For whatever technique you choose, learn about the kinds of tools, fibers, and equipment needed to accomplish the art. Collect equipment, thread, needles, scissors, hoops, etc., for your own equipment kit.

2 Find out about artists or specific styles in the technique you choose. Visit artists and see their work in progress if possible.

Share either of the above with your troop or patrol.

My signature

Leader's signature   Date badge completed

Theater

Complete six activities, including **one** of the three that are starred.

1 Read a play. Choose a character and tell:
- ☐ who this character is
- ☐ how she/he fits into the play
- ☐ what motivates this character
- ☐ what her/his objective is

2 Take a trip to a makeup center or to a place where theatrical makeup is sold. Watch a demonstration. If possible, watch the makeup being applied the night of an amateur or professional performance in your town. Learn to identify different articles of stage makeup. Make up one complete face for a special character (old man, clown, animal, etc.).

OR Create a mask to be used in a skit based on a story you have chosen.

3 Using basic ingredients (pieces of fabrics, yarn, newspapers, sheets, old clothes, costume jewelry, etc.) design your own costumes and props for a performance.

4 Attend a play, a theatrical performance, a children's theater, a puppet show, a dinner theater, or a school, church, or community play. Make an appointment ahead of time to talk with the performers after the show. Ask about their involvement with the theater. Prepare your questions before you go to the theater.

5 Find out about choral reading and choose a piece to rehearse; perform this for your troop, for another troop, or for a council occasion.

*6 Create some puppets, a shadowgraph, or marionettes and prepare for them appropriate stage sets and lighting. You might make up an original play for them, act out a folktale, or act out a story that is on a record or tape. Put on your performance for another group.

7 Try a variety of creative dramatic techniques:

- ☐ Do mirror mimic with someone else. Take turns being the leader. Don't talk. Try to express a feeling.
- ☐ Use a sentence such as "I did it." and say it five times expressing different emotions: pride, guilt, fear, happiness, surprise, horror, etc.
- ☐ Create a pantomime based on a reaction to something: taste something sweet/sour, touch something hot/cold, see something beautiful/horrible, smell something fragrant/foul.
- ☐ Portray in pantomime (choose five) a person who is: lazy, sad, energetic, happy, sick, athletic, etc.
- ☐ Pretend to have a conversation on the phone with an imaginary person.
- ☐ Do an improvisation with a small group based on suggestions from your audience.

*8 With your patrol or group, choose a familiar story. Make a list of the important events in the story. Decide which events you'll show in a scene and how many scenes you'll have. List the characters. Decide who will play each part. Make up the dialogue, movements, voices, and gestures that suit the characters. Use a narrator to present your scenes. When you're ready to act out your story scenes use simple costumes, just enough to make it clear to others what characters you're playing.

9 Prepare a pantomime performance using costumes, makeup and/or props if possible.

*10 With your troop, patrol, or small group choose a written play or scenes from a play. Produce the play with your group. Rehearse and put on your play with an audience. Each girl should do two or more of the following:

- ☐ Learn and perform the part of one character or be an understudy.
- ☐ Be the play director, stage manager, part of a directing committee, or the prompter.
- ☐ Draw a model of the stage set.
- ☐ Work out the stage directions for every action and movement.
- ☐ Create the actual stage set with backgrounds, furniture, etc.
- ☐ Collect properties, list when they are to be used, and be ready to present them on cue. Set up a prop table behind stage.
- ☐ Prepare the costumes.
- ☐ Do the makeup.
- ☐ Design and make the programs, invitations, posters, or flyers, for your play.

11 Find out about theater, puppetry, or dramatic events/pageants either historical or current in at least two countries other than your own. Find pictures, make drawings, prepare a booklet, or do a dramatic presentation to demonstrate to others what you have learned.

12 Find a short mystery thriller or science fiction play or write an original one that needs several sound effects. Put on your play with all the sound effects. Figure out and gather the props to make at least ten of these: rain on a window, thunder, dog barking, rocket launch, ocean waves on rocks, horn of an old car, car door slamming, feet on a fire escape, horses galloping, truck climbing a steep hill, helicopter in flight, foghorn from a distance, attic door opening, people running, communications from outer space (or make up your own sound effects to fit your story). The sounds can be taped ahead of time if equipment is available.

My signature

Leader's signature   Date badge completed

Visual Arts

Complete six activities, including the two starred.

1 Practice **seeing** the things you look at. Make a list of 15 different designs you find in nature (such as the spiral of a snail's shell or the pattern of leaves in a cabbage cut in half) and 15 that are man-made (such as a line of grocery carts or the parts of a bicycle).

2 Practice **seeing** the colors around you. Choose at least two scenes, such as fresh folded laundry or a hill full of trees. How many tones of green can you see in the trees and hills, how many tones of white in the laundry?

3 Learn the meaning of naturalistic, conventional, geometric, and abstract designs. Collect or draw samples of these four types. Make a simple border design using straight lines and dots. Make another using curves.

4 Make a color wheel and explain the colors to someone. Learn the primary, secondary, and complementary colors. Learn to mix at least four colors in paint. Then experiment with colors by overlaying pieces of colored tissue or acetate.

5 Look through newspapers and magazines for different kinds of lettering. Cut out samples and use them to discuss with your troop or patrol how different styles seem to make you feel differently about the letters and words. Try using lettering pens. Practice different styles of lettering. Letter a poster, brochure, or flyer for something your school, troop, or church is doing.

6 Visit one or more places where you can see many types of visual arts. The place(s) could be a museum, exhibit, art gallery, gift shop, department store, art collector's home, artist's studio, art show, or festival. If possible, visit a place where you can see an artist at work and can talk to her/him about the work you are observing. This could be a potter's studio; a printmaking shop; a weaving studio; a class in crewel, embroidery, or stitchery; or a sculptor's or painter's studio. Try to see examples of paintings, sculptures, prints, ceramics, pottery, woodwork, weaving and/or stitchery. Make a list of the art forms you like best and why.

7 Choose an art form in the visual arts and read about an artist or group of artists who worked in this medium. Share your learnings with others.

*8 Create an original work in a two-dimensional art form — a painting; a drawing in pencil, ink, or colored pen; a collage; a chalk, pastel, or mixed media design; or a print (stencil, linoleum, silk screen transfer, or monoprint). Mount your work.

OR Create a work in a three-dimensional art form — a sculpture or pottery in clay; a wood or plaster carving; a structure or form in metal, wood, or natural materials; a carving in relief; a mosaic or a diorama; a mobile; a stabile; or a paper sculpture.

OR Create a work in one or more types of textiles — a weaving on a simple loom, an embroidery design, a basket, a macrame, a quilting design, a hooked design, or other creative combination of textile arts.

Whichever activity you choose, show your work to others and be able to explain the process in your art form and the materials and tools needed to do it.

9 Collect several symbols or logos that represent places, people, or ideas. Then create your own shield (coat of arms) in a large size showing symbols of what represents you. Share with your troop or patrol.

OR After collecting symbols, create a coat of arms for a famous character. Display it at a troop or patrol meeting and see if people can guess the character.

OR Create a symbolic design for a plate, a mug, or a button. If possible, have these made.

10 Experiment with at least three interesting techniques that relate to visual arts, such as string painting, crayon etching, or other resist painting, sponge painting, finger painting, or tissue overlays.

OR Create an original game that could be enjoyed by young people your age. Use a visual technique (painting, drawing, building) to make the game or have something in the visual arts be part of the rules of the game.

11 Create at least three paintings that reflect your feelings when listening to music or after reading a poem. Try to have three different feelings in your works.

*12 Do at least two of the following:

☐ **Line:** Select two pictures that show different uses of line and explain these uses to others. Experiment with a felt tip pen or crayon to show different kinds of line (straight, curved, broken), direction of line (horizontal, vertical, diagonal), and qualities of line (thick, thin, dark, light).

☐ **Form and space:** Select two pictures that show use of shapes. Point out the basic forms — circles, squares, triangles, etc. Paint or make a collage of an abstract composition based on arrangements of form. Be able to explain negative space.

☐ **Value:** Select two pictures that show a variety of lights and darks. Explain how artists use different values to create their composition. Experiment with paint to make tints and shades of color. Create a picture using different values of one color.

☐ **Color:** Select two pictures that show an interesting, exciting, or pleasing use of color. Discuss how color can affect the appearance of things or your feelings about them. Experiment with mixing colors and create a picture in colors that expresses a word, such as spring, winter, joy, sorrow, etc.

☐ **Texture:** Select two pictures that show different uses of texture. Discuss how the texture is accomplished. Create two designs — one that uses real texture (bark, sand, cotton, etc.) and one that uses visual texture (paint strokes, pattern, crinkled paper, etc.).

My signature

Leader's signature   Date badge completed

The World of
the Out-of-Doors

Dabbler

Complete one activity in each group.

A.1 Become acquainted with a plant, such as tree, a weed, or a shrub growing in your neighborhood. Learn how this plant gets food and water. Find out what living things depend upon this plant for food and shelter. Using drawings, poetry, or photographs tell about the plant and all the living things that are included in the food chain.

  2 Make your own environmental discovery tools or collect pieces of equipment you can use to explore a pond, collect rocks, predict weather, or observe wildlife. Learn how to use them. Teach someone else how to use them to make her own discoveries.

B.1 Watch birds, insects, or other wild animals around your home and notice how they live and what they eat. Keep eco-notes of your discoveries to share with your troop.

  2 With other girls, help plan a Scouts' Own to share your feelings about wild animals around your home or far away.

C.1 Learn the following outdoor skills well enough to show someone else: how and when to tie a square knot, half hitch, and overhand knot, how to hank a rope, how to handle a knife, how to make a bedroll.

  2 With your group, plan one meal or snack that needs no cooking, or one that lets each person cook, or one that serves the whole group. Know how to build and put out a fire. Help plan, buy, carry, prepare, serve, and eat food. Help clean up.

D.1 On a hike, follow or lay a trail, follow a street or road map, or make a sketch map.

  2 Mark places on a map of your community where you can do outdoor activities and sports.

E.1 With your troop, take at least three hikes to a favorite spot. Make a list of what lives there and any changes you discover.

  2 Make something you can use when hiking, biking, camping, riding, or boating, such as a sit-upon, miser's bag, toggle, saddlebag, or lead line.

F.1 Put on a skit to show you know the buddy system, safety rules, and how to dress for outdoor trips in different kinds of weather and for the types of outdoor activities you enjoy.

  2 Play water games to demonstrate that you can float and put on a PFD (Personal Flotation Device) correctly.

G.1 Make a list of things happening in your community that hurt the environment. Do a project with your family or troop to improve your community's environment, such as planting and/or maintaining a tree to reduce air pollution.

  2 Find out what kind of eco-action is going on in the camps in your Girl Scout council. Ask what kind of projects need to be done by girls. Pick one of these projects to do the next time your group goes to camp.

My signature

Leader's signature   Date badge completed

Bicycling

Complete six activities, including the two starred.

*1 Hold an on-the-road traffic session or field day. Have participants demonstrate that they can:
- ☐ start and stop
- ☐ use a brake to control speed
- ☐ give correct hand signals
- ☐ make eye contact with drivers of trucks, cars, and other bicycles to tell them what to do and to make sure they understand
- ☐ watch for cars at intersections, alleys, and driveways
- ☐ make left turns while watching for cars and making eye contact

OR Teach someone else how to do all of the above correctly.

2 Invite a member of the traffic department or local safety council to talk to your group about bicycle safety and/or bicycle inspection or licensing.

OR Develop and carry out a plan to help young children understand how to be safe riders.

3 Hold a bicycle clinic on making basic bicycle repairs and on keeping your bicycle clean, rust free, lubricated, and properly adjusted.

OR Make a list of basic bicycle repairs and show that you know how to make them or can tell the repair mechanic what has to be done.

4 Find out the causes of the five major types of bicycle accidents in your community. With a friend, pinpoint hazards or trouble spots in your community related to these accidents. Find a way to tell others about these hazards.

5 Visit a bicycle sales department or repair shop and learn about the different types of bicycles. Find out what to look for when buying a bicycle.

OR Find out how local bicycle clubs or groups, such as the Bicycle Manufacturers Association, National Safety Council, United States Consumer Product Safety Commission, National Park Service, United States Department of Transportation, or American Youth Hostels, Inc., can help your group.

6 With others in your group, plan and carry out a troop, school, or community bicycle safety project.

OR Drive a safe bike. Have it inspected regularly. Learn defensive bicycle driving.

7 Learn how to read and follow a road map. With others in your group, mark on a road map (or make a map to show) the safest bicycle routes from your home to school, to Girl Scout meetings, to the shopping center, or to the homes of friends.

OR Plan and take part in three bicycle adventures to discover historical homes, museums, or parks within easy reach of the cyclists in your community. Make a map and trail guide for others to use in visiting one of these places.

8 Ask an experienced cyclist in your area to tell you how to take care of and ride a bicycle on a trip or how to plan for a bicycle trip.

OR Make a personal first aid kit, foul weather kit, and tool kit for emergency repairs to fasten on your bicycle. Know how to be prepared for unexpected weather in your area and where to seek shelter from a sudden storm.

9 Pack a bicycle saddlebag or show how to carry your gear safely when bicycling to school, to the grocery store, or on an all-day or overnight bicycle trip.

*10 With your group, go on an all-day bicycle trip, using different routes to go to and return from your destination. Help plan when and where to go, the purpose of the trip, the route, what to take, what to wear, permissions needed, and a nutritious sack lunch suitable for the occasion.

OR With your group go on an overnight bicycle trip. Help plan when and where to go; the route; what to take, eat, and wear; and permissions needed.

My signature

Leader's signature   Date badge completed

Boating

Complete six activities, including the three starred.

*1 Show that you can use and care for a PFD (Personal Flotation Device).
- ☐ Tell when PFDs should be worn and who needs to wear them.
- ☐ Tell from the label if a PFD is Coast Guard approved, the right type, and the right size.
- ☐ Adjust a life jacket or life vest to fit.
- ☐ Throw and float with a buoyant cushion or life ring.
- ☐ Stow PFDs in a handy place on a boat or ashore.
- ☐ Tell if a PFD is in good condition.
- ☐ Float, swim, and do HELP (Heat Escape Lessening Position) and huddle in a PFD. (For instructions see Water Fun, activity 1.)
- ☐ Put on a PFD in water that's over your head, if you're a swimmer.

2 Be able to keep a boat in trim. Show that you can:
- ☐ Prevent a boat from being overloaded.
- ☐ Stow things and move weight around safely.
- ☐ Keep water from rising or sloshing around in the bottom of the boat.

3 Show that you can handle a small craft safely. In a rowboat, canoe, sailboat, or motorboat:
- ☐ Get underway.
- ☐ Make turns and go straight.
- ☐ Speed up, slow down, and stop.
- ☐ Secure the craft.

4 Keep a sharp lookout. Show that you practice boating rules of the road as you:
- ☐ Keep away from swimmers, divers, and people fishing.
- ☐ Look out for other boats, floating objects, or dangers under the surface.
- ☐ Spot helps like buoys, lights, or landmarks.
- ☐ Help someone in distress or signal for help yourself.
- ☐ Watch out for wakes.
- ☐ Treat the water habitat with care.

5 Do your share to keep a boat **shipshape**. Do at least **three** of the following:
   - [ ] Unload or stow gear or rigging.
   - [ ] Wash down, bail out, or sponge off.
   - [ ] Scrub, sand, scrape, or chip.
   - [ ] Paint, patch, or fix up.
   - [ ] Tie knots, splice, or whip lines.
   - [ ] Make something to add to boating comfort.

*6 Be ready for boating emergencies. Go over what to do if:
   - [ ] you fall overboard
   - [ ] someone else falls in
   - [ ] the wind rises (or, if sailing, dies)
   - [ ] waters get rough
   - [ ] the boat swamps or capsizes
   - [ ] it gets dark or foggy
   - [ ] there's a fire on board

7 Be a water and weather watcher. To tell if it's safe to be out in a boat, show you can take cues from:
   - [ ] wind direction and speed
   - [ ] waves, tides, or currents
   - [ ] clouds
   - [ ] weather reports or signals

8 Take care of comfort afloat. Model what you should wear to prevent harm from:
   - [ ] the sun
   - [ ] the wind
   - [ ] cold temperatures
   - [ ] wet conditions

   Show that you know how to recognize and treat someone who:
   - [ ] is not breathing
   - [ ] has sunburn, heat stroke, heat exhaustion
   - [ ] has hypothermia
   - [ ] is seasick

9 Ahoy! Be an "old salt" by doing at least **two** of the following:
   - [ ] Use the nautical terms for the major parts of a boat.
   - [ ] Point out different types of boats for different uses.
   - [ ] Tell time from ship's bells or a 24-hour clock.
   - [ ] Find out some everyday phrases that have nautical origins.
   - [ ] Learn your name in international code flags, Morse code, or phonetic alphabet.
   - [ ] Swap sea stories or chanteys.

10 Find out about people who "go down to the sea in ships."
- ☐ Look back at life at sea before 1900.
- ☐ Look into what it's like to be a crew member, a scientist, or a captain at sea today.
- ☐ Imagine life on a ship in the future.

*11 Add at least three important items to this safe boating checklist.
- ☐ Have a PFD on board for each person.
- ☐ File a float plan.
- ☐
- ☐
- ☐

Before you get underway, be in charge of seeing that everything on your list is done right.

12 Launch a day-long adventure by boat, or be in a boat parade, regatta, or race. On a chart or map, figure out:
- ☐ what course you'll follow or what landmarks you can expect to see along the way
- ☐ how far you'll go
- ☐ how long it will take
- ☐ where you could find refuge in an emergency

My signature

Leader's signature   Date badge completed

Eco-Action

Complete four activities, including the one starred.

1 Find out how to read your electric meter. Compile a list of the items in your home that use electricity. Which appliances use it at a fast rate? Find out how the electricity you use is made. In order to save energy, how could you use less electricity or none at all? Poll your family to find out how they would use less or none. Develop a family energy conservation plan and measure your results.

2 How many cans, bottles, aluminum items, papers, and plastics does your family throw away in a week? Where does the trash go? Take four different items of trash and cut a strip about 2 cm × 6 cm (about ¾ in. × 2¼ in.) of each. Bury the strips separately in soil in a container. Keep the soil moist and remove the strips each week. Is there any decay? Make a chart and keep a record of what happens over a month or two. Which items will decay fastest or slowest when thrown away?

3 Find a safe corner in your area where you can make a traffic survey. Count the number of vehicles that pass by in 30 minutes at three different times of day. How many people are there in each vehicle? Think of ways to save energy and move people more efficiently.

4 Check out your local streams or waterways for pollution for a month. Take a water sample. Record signs of oil on water and color of the water. Take a walk around your neighborhood and make a list of the things that will be washed by rainfall into nearby streams or lakes.

OR Every day for two weeks record the air quality in your community. Can you smell the air? taste it? see for a long distance? Record the temperature, time of day, and amount of wind. Coat a heavy piece of paper with petroleum jelly. Put it outside on a level spot. Observe it for specks of air pollution that fall onto it.

What are the sources of water and air pollution in your community? Do you contribute to any of these?

5 During or after a heavy rain, walk around your neighborhood or campsite and look for signs of soil being carried away, such as gullies in a soil bank or muddy water. On a windy day, look for spots without plants and observe what the wind is doing to the soil.

Why is it important to conserve the soil we have? Find out how farmers prevent soil erosion or how soil erosion can be prevented on a construction site.

Find an eroded site where you can help keep the soil in place. Plan and carry out an improvement project. Watch carefully to see the results of your project.

6 Locate an area in your community where you think trees play an important role in the environment. Do they provide shade, beauty, a wind and sound barrier, or protection from soil erosion? What kinds of trees grow in the area you found? What difficulties do trees have growing in your area?

Plan a project to help a tree by watering, fertilizing, etc., or plant a new tree and provide the things it needs to grow.

*7 An environmental problem is caused by something humans have added or done to the environment. Find a problem that you could do something about and some people interested in working with you to help.
- [ ] Learn all you can about the problem.
- [ ] Evaluate the possible solutions.
- [ ] Develop a plan of action.
- [ ] Act on your plan.
- [ ] Evaluate what happened.

My signature

Leader's signature

Date badge completed

Ecology

Complete three activities, including the two starred.

*1 Ecology is the study of plants and animals and their environment (ecosystems). Choose an area near where you live or at camp, that you would like to learn more about (for example, a seashore, grassland, marsh, pond, river, or forest). After exploring the area:

- ☐ Make a list of the plants and animals that live there.
- ☐ Draw a diagram to show the different layers of plant life in the area. Try to figure out why these occur.
- ☐ Dig into the soil and draw a picture of its layers. Tell what each layer is made of.
- ☐ Using a thermometer, take at least 30 readings in the area to find the warmest and coolest places. Or, make a rain gauge to measure the rainfall in the area for one month.
- ☐ Tell how soil, rain, temperature, and wind affect the plants and animals in your area.

2 Learn how food and energy are passed through an ecosystem by imagining what you would do if you were given 50 acres of soil. What would you plant and what animals would you raise before you could bake the cookies in your favorite recipe?

Make a list of each of:

- ☐ the producers on your farm, that is the plants that use sunlight, water, and minerals to make food
- ☐ the herbivores—the plant eaters
- ☐ the carnivores—the meat eaters
- ☐ the decomposers (How will the leftovers be recycled back into the environment?)

How will you and the other herbivores, carnivores, and decomposers use the energy you get from the food you eat?

3 Find out how wildlife communities change.

Plants and animals can change the ecosystem around them. A tree may add chemicals to the soil and shade its surroundings so that even its own seedlings cannot grow nearby. Other plants and animals will move in to take advantage of the new conditions. This process is called **succession.**

Find five examples of succession, such as:
- ☐ tree seedlings beginning to grow from a bed of lichens and ferns
- ☐ an unmown lawn or vacant lot being taken over by weeds
- ☐ lichens changing conditions on the rock face
- ☐ shrubs or young trees multiplying in an abandoned field
- ☐ aquatic plants growing into areas of open water

OR Find two examples of how animal or plant populations (numbers) change.
- ☐ Using an insect sweep net, sweep through a grassy area and count the kinds and numbers of insects captured. Do the same thing several weeks later. What are the differences?
- ☐ Keep track of the kinds and numbers of birds coming to a feeding station over several months. What are the differences during these months?
- ☐ Visit a place where you can see migrating animals and learn about their journey and changing numbers.
- ☐ Visit a place where you can see how the kinds and numbers of plants and animals change as elevation changes or distance from water changes.
- ☐ Visit a place that has been changed by fire. How were the plants and animals affected?

4 Look for the special features that each plant and animal has to help it do its job in the ecosystem.

One of the jobs of each plant is to produce and scatter its young. Find examples of five ways plants produce new plants or structures that help spread the seeds. What special features help them do this?

OR Find out how your teeth are different from those of a dog or cat or other mammal. What can you tell about an animal's diet by looking at the kinds of teeth it has?

OR Watch an animal that is eating. Describe the ways that it keeps alert to other things around it. How would this behavior help it survive?

*5 To show how living things live together, construct a balanced terrarium or aquarium containing producers, consumers, and decomposers. Record how things in this ecosystem affect each other. Tell how the water, oxygen, and carbon dioxide move through this ecosystem. Tell why a source of light is needed for life.

OR Describe the ways in which the earth is like a manned spaceship. Tell how water, carbon, oxygen, and carbon dioxide are recycled on earth. As a crew member on spaceship earth, decide what you can do to stretch out the use of our supplies and help ecosystems do their work.

OR Do a project that will help an ecosystem survive.

My signature

Leader's signature   Date badge completed

Finding Your Way

Complete eight activities, including the three starred.

*1 Locate as many different types of maps and charts as you can that include the area where you live, your state capital, or an area you wish to visit. Use the maps to tell about the area.

OR Pretend that you need to explain what a map is to someone who speaks your language but has never heard of a map before. Using at least four of the maps you have collected, explain what maps are and the information each map gives.

*2 Know the length of your pace. Find out how long it takes you to walk 1.6 km (about 1 mile) comfortably over fairly level ground, then figure out how long at this rate it should take you to walk the distance between two points you have marked on a map.

3 Draw a sketch map of your route to school, to a shopping center, or to a favorite spot. Ask someone to test your map by following it. Draw a second sketch map based upon the description someone gives you of the route to school or some place of interest. Together, follow your map to see if it is correct. In both maps, include compass directions and a legend (key) explaining the symbols you used.

4 Draw a map of your campsite or your neighborhood locating land-marks, streets, paths or trails, bodies of water, and other details. Include a legend (key) to explain the symbols you used, compass direction, scale, and other information.

*5 Show that you know how to use a compass by:
☐ explaining how to adjust the difference between true and mag-netic north
☐ setting a given bearing and following it a short distance
☐ sighting on an object, going to it, and returning to your starting point

OR Teach someone else how to use a compass.

6 Show how to find the four cardinal points by using the sun, stars, or other natural signs.

OR Tell what natural signs a group that has lost the trail might use to find its way home.

7 Develop an indoor/outdoor game or activity for small spaces that could help others learn how to use a compass.

8 Make a three-dimensional model of a portion of a topographical map to show contour intervals of the hills and valleys.

OR Using half of a potato to represent a hill, make a topographical map of the potato to show its contours.

9 Plan an imaginary orienteering hike with at least six stations. Draw the route you would take between stations and what you would see along the way.

OR Plot a course with at least six legs (stations) on a nautical chart or map. Then chart the route you would take between each two points, locating the navigation aids and landmarks that you would see along the way.

10 With others, set up a miniature compass walk in a nearby park or campsite.

OR Take part in a map and compass clinic or orienteering event in your area.

My signature

Leader's signature   Date badge completed

Foot Traveler

Complete six activities, including the one starred.

*1 With your group, plan and go on at least four walking trips in or near your community. One of the trips should be at least 3 km (about 2 miles) long. Another of the trips should be on a hiking trail in a park or in open country. Plan the routes, get necessary permissions, come dressed for expected weather and the kind of hike.

2 Know how to walk and rest correctly, how to walk in a group on a street, highway, trail, or country road.

3 On one hike use a street or road map to find your way. On another hike, sketch a map of the route taken. On one hike, learn how to use a compass with a map.

OR Lay a trail, using at least four different trail signs and follow successfully a trail laid by others.

4 Plan and pack a well-balanced, easy-to-carry snack or lunch for each hike. Know what foods cause thirst and those that quench thirst. On one hike, prepare a hot drink using a Buddy burner and a tin can stove or a portable (backpacker) stove.

5 Dress for the expected weather and activities. Pack a day pack or shoulder bag large enough to hold the essentials you will need for day hikes or walking trips.

OR Make a piece of hiking equipment for yourself. For example, sew a day pack, decorate a hike stick, weave a sit-upon, make a Buddy burner and tin can stove, or improvise a poncho.

6 Help keep a first aid kit ready for use on hikes. Know how to bandage a sprained ankle and care for a skinned knee blister, an insect bite, a cut, and sunburn or windburn. Know health and safety practices for day hikes and how to get help in an emergency.

7 Help make a list of interesting places within a radius of 3 km (about 2 miles) of your troop meeting place. Write down the directions for reaching each site, the time it will take to walk there, and what to see and do at the site. Include information on fees, hours open, nearby picnic and toilet facilities. Find a way to share this information with others in your neighborhood.

OR Find out about the organized groups in your community interested in walking and day hiking. Attend one of their meetings or ask someone from one of the groups to come and tell your group about their activities. Find out if you can take part in any of their special projects.

8 Teach your group a new hiking song or a game to play along the way.

OR Find a way to share your joy of walking with others. This might be by taking some other group on one of your walking adventures, by finding or writing a poem, story, or picture to describe how you feel.

9 Organize or take part in a project to clean up a trail or walkway in or near your community.

OR Organize or take part in a trail-building project. This might be an urban trail, a measured mile, a three senses nature trail, a jogging path, a physical fitness trail, or a wheelchair route through your community.

My signature

Leader's signature   Date badge completed

Hiker

Take a series of hikes that together will total at least 40 km (25 miles) and complete eight activities, including the three starred.

1 On one of your hikes, organize girls in your group as an exploring party with a leader, navigator, cartographer, botanist, geologist, log keeper, photographer or artist, and an outfitter and explore an unfamiliar trail.

2 On a road map of your area, locate all hiking trails with access or exit spots located within 40 km (25 miles) of your home. Find out what permissions are required to hike on them. Plan to take a hike on one of these trails.

*3 Know how to dress and what to take with you on a hike or overnight hiking trip. On one of your day hikes, take part in a wide game or act out a situation where you and others in your group must improvise a shelter for the night and improvise bodily protection from heat, cold, wind, rain, or snow.

*4 With others in your group, talk about hiking health and safety. Make a list of the most important things to remember and what your group can do to be safety-wise. Know how to get emergency help on a hike and first aid treatment for serious bleeding, hypothermia, frostbite, heat exhaustion, and shock.

5 Use a compass and topographic map to lay out a cross-country hike and help a group follow this trail.

OR Complete activity 5 of the Finding Your Way badge.

6 Show someone what to take and how to pack a knapsack for an overnight hiking trip. Demonstrate how to erect a simple trail shelter or to put up a trail tent.

OR On an overnight hike, carry a knapsack containing everything you need and your share of the group's general equipment. With your buddy, erect and strike a trail shelter or trail tent. Show your appreciation of the out-of-doors by leaving your campsite better than you found it.

7 Know how to select, pack, carry, and prepare food for overnight and all-day hikes. Help plan and prepare meals for at least two of your hiking trips. Include at least one no-cook cold weather meal or one hot meal prepared on a backpacker stove or Buddy burner and tin can stove.

OR Prepare, taste-test, and package a homemade backpacker's food or mix for your group's use.

8 Find out about the Appalachian Trail, the Pacific Crest Trail, and a national scenic or historic trail located in your area. Find out what you can do to help with their upkeep and repair.

OR Help others become aware of good hiking practices and the need for trails near your community.

*9 Help your group plan and go on two all-day hikes or an overnight hiking trip to a council-approved site. Plan where to go, what to wear, and what to take. Find out about hiking, camping, and fire regulations you must observe and why. Get necessary permissions and arrange for at-home emergency contact and transportation.

My signature

Leader's signature   Date badge completed

Horseback Rider

Complete seven activities, including the two starred.

1 Saddle and bridle a horse by yourself. Explain the care and use of each part of the tack and the importance of correct fitting. Hitch a horse at the correct height when bridled, using a halter or rope, a suitable knot, and the correct length of rope.

2 Visit a harness or tack shop or obtain a harness catalog and become acquainted with different styles of saddles, bridles, and bits. Find out the advantages of each type and know the approximate cost. Teach someone else how to clean and care for tack.

3 Find out about the breeding and training of horses used in your community, such as police horses, cavalry horses, race horses, or dray horses.

*4 Demonstrate that you can do the following in good form: mount and dismount correctly; turn and stop a horse, at walk and at trot, on command; post at trot; back up, circle, and canter in good form either from the halt or the walk.

5 Explain safety regulations for riding and equestrian etiquette. Show how to give proper hand signals when riding on public roads and how to do an emergency dismount at halt and at walk. Tell what to do if your horse rears, trips, bucks, stops, or bolts.

6 Illustrate by demonstration or pictures the correct and safe clothing for horse shows, western trail rides, hunts, and your group's own equestrian activities. Point out to others the safety features to look for in the footwear, pants, jackets, and safety hat you wear when riding.

7 Name the principal parts of a horse. Find out from the veterinarian or horse trainer what can be done to prevent the common ailments or diseases of horses.

8 Find out where there are suitable trails for horseback riding in your area. Help with the care and maintenance of one of these bridle trails.

OR Name the tools used for grooming a horse. Demonstrate the use of each one. Learn how to care for a horse after exercising.

*9 Help someone you know to feel comfortable around horses and understand the need for safety precautions on the trail or in the ring, stable, or pasture.

OR Help someone earn her Horse Lover badge.

10 Collect cowboy ballads and teach one to your troop.

OR Learn about famous or legendary horses. Tell a horse story to your troop or another group.

11 Plan and take part in a trail breakfast, a supper ride, or a troop demonstration of riding skills.

OR Take a trip to a state or county fair to see the horse show. If possible, enter a show class that is right for you and your horse.

OR Attend a local horse show. If possible, serve as an usher, runner, or in some other capacity that will help the show run smoothly.

12 Plan and carry out a gymkhana for your troop. You may also wish to invite another troop or other riders 11 years old or younger to participate.

My signature

Leader's signature   Date badge completed

Horse Lover

Complete six activities, including the two starred.

*1 Find out where you can ride in your community. Ask each group or facility how much it charges for membership, riding, or riding lessons. Find out whether its specialty is English or Western riding and which groups provide instruction, which require you to own your own horse, which have indoor and outdoor rings, and which have riding trails.

*2 Visit a stable. Find out from the owner or manager what is involved in the care of a horse. Find out how much and what kind of food a horse needs daily, acceptable treats for horses, everyday care for a stable, how often a horse needs to be shod and why. If possible, watch while a farrier pulls and resets a shoe.

3 Examine the tools used to groom a horse. Discover the purpose of each. Learn to use the brush and currycomb. Practice safe stall and barn behavior. Find out how to cool a horse after riding.

4 Learn the parts of a saddle and a bridle. Find out how each part contributes to the comfort of the horse and rider. Learn how to take care of a saddle and bridle for long wear and good repair.

5 Watch or assist with the saddling and bridling of a horse. Be able to explain to someone else what is being done and the use of each piece of equipment.

OR Saddle and bridle the horse you are going to ride.

6 Take enough riding lessons to learn the basics of ring riding, how to: mount and dismount, ride at a walk, back up, trot, guide a horse while riding, and with supervision, lead a horse to the stable.

OR Demonstrate to other horse lovers how to mount and dismount, ride at a walk and a trot. Show others how to groom a horse and how to care for a horse after exercising.

7 Be a safe rider. Learn how to dismount abruptly at a walk and a trot. Explain regulations for riding and good ring manners. Know how to dress for Western or English riding.

8 Find out how to use your natural aids — your hands, your legs, your weight, and your voice — to tell your horse what to do. Know how to get along with horses in the stable and in the ring or pasture.

9 Make an illustrated booklet about the history and development of the horse. Be able to point out and name the principal parts of a horse.

OR Collect or take photographs of four breeds that interest you. Tell or write about their distinctive features and use.

10 Read one or more books about horses. These might include books on horsemanship, information on related careers, stories about famous horses, or stories of adventure on horseback.

11 Find out about the groups in your community who share your love for horses and might help you and others increase your skills and knowledge.

OR Attend a traveling performance of horses from the Spanish Riding School or some other performance by show riders, such as a rodeo, a local horse show, or a draft horse pulling contest.

12 Go on a breakfast or supper trail ride or a short cross-country ride.

OR Take part in an appropriate class in a horse show.

My signature

Leader's signature   Date badge completed

Outdoor Cook

Complete eight activities, including the four starred.

*1 With four to eight other people help plan, prepare, and serve four different inexpensive outdoor meals, using a different type of cooking in each meal. Help do at least one of the following for each meal: plan the menu, make shopping and equipment lists, shop, pack, take care of the food at the cookout site, establish an eating place, prepare and serve the food, or clean up including dishwashing.

2 Find a few recipes from your own region or recipes from at least three different countries or cultures, using a common food, such as beans, rice, or potatoes. Prepare one of these recipes during a cookout.

*3 Set up and use four different types of cooking fires, including charcoal. Explain the advantages of each, and when to use or not to use it. Know how to put out cooking fires safely and demonstrate this when you have finished using each fire you built. Find out the regulations in your community for building cooking fires in backyards, in parks, or on public properties.

4 Make and use a cooking fire for windy or wet weather.

OR Demonstrate how to use a backpacker's stove or camp stove safely by preparing food on it for yourself and your group.

*5 On one of the cookouts, take charge of one part of the cleanup. Show that you can put out the fire, wash, and sanitize your dishes; and dispose of the garbage, paper, tin cans, and glass without endangering the environment.

6 Make a personal cook kit, a Buddy burner and tin can stove, or a charcoal stove. Use it to prepare food for yourself by boiling, baking, toasting, and frying.

OR Help collect or make items for a troop, group, or patrol kitchen box or kit. Pack the equipment in a box or sack that one or two people in your group can easily transport.

7 Help plan and package a tasty, easy-to-pack, high-energy dinner for a hot weather meal needing no refrigeration that you could take with you for emergency use when cooking fires are not permitted.

8 Be a supermarket sleuth. With one or more friends, check out your grocery store for tasty, inexpensive lightweight foods that do not need refrigeration or long cooking time and that are suitable for cookouts and camping trips. See who can get the longest list. At home or in a cookout meal, taste-test one item you are not familiar with.

OR Experiment by preparing and packaging your own dry mixes for trailside cooking.

OR Sun dry or oven dry some fresh fruit, vegetables, or seasonings to use on a cookout.

9 Bake something in a cardboard oven or in a tin can stove over a Buddy burner or bake something in the coals.

OR Use a hay box, hay hole, or thermos jug to prepare a slow-cooked meal.

10 Practice measuring dry, liquid, and solid ingredients until you can judge amounts without standard measuring tools.

*11 Share your skills with others. Teach someone or some group how to build a type of fire new to them, to cook something over it, to put out the fire, and clean it up.

My signature

Leader's signature   Date badge completed

Outdoor Fun

Complete six activities, including the one starred.

*1 Help your troop, patrol, or family plan and carry out three daytime outings. Before you go, find out what equipment is at each site, such as outdoor stoves, picnic tables, shelters, and sports equipment. Make a list of the group and personal equipment to take.

2 With others, help plan, buy, pack, carry, prepare, and serve a different meal or snack for each outing, such as one that needs no cooking, one that lets each person cook her own, and one you cook for the group. Help clean up after each meal or snack.

3 Show you can make a basic fire, prepare food on it, put it out, and leave the fire site in good condition.

4 Help plan, assemble, and pack a first aid kit for your outdoor activities. Know first aid for burns and cuts and tell ways you can prevent accidents in the out-of-doors.

5 Plan games, songs, and campfires for each outing that are especially suitable for the season or the site.

6 Know how to dispose of waste water and garbage without damaging the environment. Learn how to sanitize your dishes in the out-of-doors and keep them clean.

7 Find ways to use a square knot and the clove hitch on one of your outings. Learn a new knot or hitch that you can use when you go troop camping or on your next outdoor day.

OR Make shavings and a toggle with a jackknife.

OR Make and use two pieces of outdoor cooking equipment.

8 Plan a skit showing what to do in outdoor emergencies and how to prevent or avoid them. Demonstrate what a lost camper should do to help others find her.

9 Help to unpack and store your troop or group's equipment after each outing. Talk over how the trip went, the things you learned that will be useful when you go out again, the things you would do differently another time, and the new things you want to do next time.

My signature

Leader's signature   Date badge completed

Swimming

Complete six activities, including the two starred.

*1 Go over ways to help yourself in case you accidentally fall in or get in trouble in the water. Show that you know when and how to:
- ☐ use a PFD (Personal Flotation Device)
- ☐ cooperate with someone who is trying to rescue you
- ☐ keep afloat with clothing and other aids
- ☐ use good sense in cold water, in deep water, in a current, and in rough waters

*2 Make the buddy system really work every time you swim.
- ☐ Use or fix up a buddy board.
- ☐ Pair off swimmers of equal ability.
- ☐ Practice buddy calls until every pair of buddies gets together instantly.

3 Show that you can breathe with an easy rhythm. For two minutes, take breaths while you bob up and down in water over your own depth or turn your head to breathe while you float face down.

4 Look at ways other living things move through the water. Watch for fins that paddle, tails that swish, legs that scurry, feet that ooze, and creatures that are jet propelled. Imitate animal actions in a water game that you make up.

5 Show that you can move through the water with ease:
- ☐ Glide (2 meters).
- ☐ Kick (6 meters).
- ☐ Arm stroke (6 meters).
- ☐ Crawl, elementary backstroke, sidestroke, or breaststroke (Do two of these strokes, 25 meters each).

6 Show that you can help a swimmer who:
- ☐ has a cramp
- ☐ is shivering from hypothermia
- ☐ is not breathing
- ☐ has a sunburn, heat stroke, or heat exhaustion
- ☐ is tired

7 Make a water safety checklist that includes ways to avoid:
- ☐ falling in
- ☐ underwater hazards
- ☐ problems on ice
- ☐ polluting water that you swim in

8 Look under the surface. Show that you can do a surface dive or dive from a deck, swim under water, and bring up something from the bottom.

OR Practice safe snorkeling without disturbing the water habitat. Show that you can choose a mask that fits your face and put it on so it won't fog.

9 Show easy entry into the water in two different dives from a low board or deck. Check water depth and hazards first.

10 Get involved in swimming competition.
- ☐ Build up your speed and stamina on a team.
- ☐ Learn about swimming stars and their records.
- ☐ Be able to follow the rules for starting, turning, timing, and scoring.

11 Participate in a water show, swim meet, play day, or pageant on the water. Share your enthusiasm by inviting others to the water event. Give them tips on what to look forward to so they're sure to enjoy themselves.

My signature

Leader's signature   Date badge completed

Troop Camper

Complete at least eight activities, including the two starred.

*1 Help plan and carry out a camping trip to a cabin, tent unit, or cottage for at least two nights. Plan when and how to go, what to take and wear, what to do, what permissions are needed. Know something about the site and what is provided there. Help plan how to pay for the camping trip.

2 Before you go, make a schedule for activities, meals, free time, bedtime, setting up and closing camp. Make a kaper chart that gives each girl a turn at different camp jobs.

3 Plan well-balanced menus that fit your budget, including at least one meal cooked out over an open fire. Help shop for, pack, carry, store, prepare, or serve the food. Help clean up after a meal, using sanitary and ecological dishwashing and garbage disposal methods.

4 Help make lists of troop and personal equipment to take with you to camp. Help pack and carry the equipment and supplies.

OR Make something for your own or group use at camp, such as a knapsack, stove sack or food sack, Buddy burner, fire starter, or sit-upon.

5 Know how to use the buddy system and make a plan to use it while camping. Talk about safety and courtesy when riding in cars or buses.

OR Plan and carry out a fire or evacuation drill while camping.

6 With others in your group look for ways in which plants and animals help each other and places where the environment has been upset.

OR Learn to recognize plants and animals on the campsite that may be harmful and know what to do about them.

OR Make and/or take aids, such as a camera, sketch pad or notebook, dip net, waterscope, star map, compass, or nature guide to help you find your way, to make discoveries, and to record what you discover at camp.

7 Be alert for eco-action. Consider the environment as you use water and fire, hike, pitch tents, do crafts, play games, cook, and keep clean. Do an outdoor good turn by eliminating litter, erosion, or other human-caused problems or devise ways to warn campers of natural hazards, such as poisonous plants and animals, rock slides, or flooding.

8 With a buddy, be responsible for a flag ceremony, quiet game, campfire program, star-gazing evening, Scouts' Own, something to do while traveling, or an activity to do when an unexpected change in the weather keeps you under cover.

OR Lead a tour or hike to locate points of interest and boundaries of the site.

9 Learn a skill to use at future camping events, such as pitching a tent, orienteering, lashing, backpacking, purifying water, or cooking in a way new to you.

10 Leave the site in good condition, unpack and store troop or patrol equipment properly, return borrowed items, pay bills, and write thank-you notes to those who helped make the trip possible.

*11 (Do this activity last.) Make a list of camping tips to share with new campers and to help you the next time. Write down what you discovered about yourself and the out-of-doors and what you hope to do when you go camping again.

My signature

Leader's signature

Date badge completed

Water Fun

Complete six activities, including the two starred.

*1 Show how to use a PFD (Personal Flotation Device):
- ☐ Put it on, fit, and fasten it.
- ☐ Float and swim with it on.
- ☐ Practice HELP (Heat Escape Lessening Position) and a huddle to keep warm. (In HELP, the most important thing is to keep your head out of the water; then protect the sides of your chest with your arms, cross your ankles to keep your legs together, and if possible, raise your knees to protect your groin. It's easy to do when sitting on land, but you need to be wearing a PFD to hold the position in water. To huddle, you and a few others hold each other close, to preserve body heat and keep up group spirit, too!)

*2 Make up and play some games in the water to show you are good at the buddy system.

3 Whet your senses in the water world. Tune in at least three of your senses and:
- ☐ Listen to the sounds of the sea or a babbling brook.
- ☐ Watch the waves or a flowing stream.
- ☐ Smell salt air or taste fresh spring water.
- ☐ Feel a breeze under sail or fly a kite at the beach.
- ☐ Bury your feet in the sand or dangle them in a pool.

Then express your own feelings or enjoy music, art, or words that others have created about water.

4 Without going in yourself, show ways to help someone in trouble in water. Safely practice:
- ☐ reaching with things like a towel, pole, or human chain
- ☐ throwing objects to help someone keep afloat
- ☐ ways to do ice rescues

5 Search for signs of life or change at water's edge. Without disturbing nature's balance, do at least one of the following:
- ☐ Pick up shells, pebbles, or driftwood.
- ☐ Dig clay or build a sand castle.
- ☐ Press seaweed or pond plants.
- ☐ Visit an aquarium, aquafarm, or nature center.
- ☐ Make up your own shoreline activity.

6 Show how to get into and out of a small boat safely. Show how to keep the boat in trim (balanced) as you:
   - [ ] Load gear.
   - [ ] Stow things.
   - [ ] Move around.
   - [ ] Sit down and get up.

7 Live at least one bit of a sailor's life:
   - [ ] Tie a fancy knot.
   - [ ] Cook up some portable soup and hardtack.
   - [ ] Sail a model boat.
   - [ ] Tell direction by the stars.
   - [ ] Walk the deck of an historic ship or visit a maritime museum.
   - [ ] Launch your own nautical lore activity.

8 Keep yourself comfortable even when you're wet or perspiring. To see how you can keep warm when it's cold and wet or cool when it's hot, try out the following:
   - [ ] clothing made of wool, cotton, or synthetic materials
   - [ ] clothing in dark colors and clothing in light colors
   - [ ] different kinds of hats

9 Show that you care about clean water. List ways you can save water and not add to pollution. Then make it an everyday habit to be a clean-water-saver.

10 Use smooth moves and easy breathing as you show how well you can swim.
   - [ ] Float for one minute.
   - [ ] Demonstrate two different strokes.
   - [ ] Tread water for two minutes.
   - [ ] Swim ten meters.

11 Go to a water event like a canoe race, swim meet, surfing competition, fishing derby, gam, parade of sail, water ballet, or water ski show. Get someone to go along who will point out special things to look for and help you share the excitement.

12 Tour a place where people go to have fun on the water, such as a marina, pool, boardwalk, ferry terminal, cruise ship, party boat dock, or boat landing. Talk to someone who works there and find out what they do that helps others enjoy the water.

My signature

Leader's signature   Date badge completed

Wildlife

Complete five activities, including the three starred.

*1 Name the things all plants and animals must have to live. Tell what a habitat is. Visit a nature center, wildlife refuge, recreation area, park, or wildlife management area. Find out if and how the area is managed for wildlife.

*2 Know the poisonous plants in your locality and where each is most likely to be found. Know what to do if you touch a poisonous plant and how to act if you see a poisonous animal.

*3 Find out which bird, tree, and flower has been chosen to represent your state. Find out why each was chosen.

4 Insects:
- ☐ Learn what makes insects different from other living things.
- ☐ Learn to identify ten species.
- ☐ Learn about the life cycles of a mosquito, a grasshopper, and a butterfly or moth. Try to raise one of these insects.
- ☐ Learn about a colonial insect and what different members of the group do, or watch an insect build its nest.

5 Mammals:
- ☐ Tell what makes mammals different from other living things.
- ☐ Identify five species of wild mammals in your area.
- ☐ Learn about the life history of one mammal from each of these groups: those that fly, that live underground, that live on land, that live in water, that live in trees.
- ☐ Find out which mammals are protected by the laws of your state and the federal government.

6 Birds:
- [ ] Tell what makes birds different from other living things.
- [ ] Identify at least five birds in your area. Recognize them by song, flight pattern, or other special behavior. Tell whether each one is closest in size to a sparrow, robin, or crow.
- [ ] Find out how and why birds are protected by law.
- [ ] Try to watch a bird build a nest. Tell what materials are used in the building, or plant a garden for birds.

7 Reptiles and amphibians:
- [ ] Learn what makes reptiles and amphibians different from other living things.
- [ ] Tell the differences between reptiles and amphibians.
- [ ] Learn to recognize at least five species in your area.
- [ ] Learn which can be handled.
- [ ] Learn how and where the young are born and what they eat.
- [ ] Learn which ones are protected by law in your state.

8 Fish:
- [ ] Learn to recognize at least five species of fish in your area.
- [ ] Learn what each one eats and what eats it.
- [ ] Learn about the life of one fish in each of these groups: bony fish, fish with cartilage skeleton, lamprey.
- [ ] Visit a fish hatchery or aquarium and find out what laws protect fish, or set up a balanced aquarium and maintain it for a month.

9 Trees and woody plants:
- [ ] Learn to identify ten species in your area.
- [ ] Think about what would happen to the trees in your area in a fire, flood, or windstorm.
- [ ] Plant and care for a tree.
- [ ] Find out if any trees are protected by law in your state.
- [ ] Watch the formation of buds and leaves. Mark and measure one year's growth, or do a rubbing of a stump and determine how old the tree was when it died.

10 Herbaceous plants:
- ☐ Learn to recognize ten wild plants in your area. Learn about the habitat of each.
- ☐ Learn two ways that flowers are fertilized or that plants reproduce.
- ☐ Learn how the seeds of five plants are dispersed.
- ☐ Find out what plants are protected by law in your state.
- ☐ Grow a plant from a seed and record its growth for one month or watch a flower outdoors and record what comes to visit it.

11 Design your own category (fungi, lichens, mosses, whales, spiders, sea shells, etc.)
- ☐ Learn what makes the category different from other living things.
- ☐ Learn to identify some species by size, shape, or some other distinguishing mark. Learn about their habits, life cycle, diet, and reproduction. Make something to attract, protect, or observe your category.
- ☐ Know the state and federal laws that protect your category.
- ☐ Find out if any species are in danger of extinction and if anything is being done to help it survive.

My signature

Leader's signature   Date badge completed

Our Own Troop's Badge

When you and other members of your troop have an interest that is not included in any of the badges in this book, you can develop a special Our Own Troop's badge on that topic. An individual girl cannot do this badge by herself. A group must make up the activities, the name, and the symbol together. No other troop can use your badge. Even if they choose the same subject, they must create their own activities and symbol.

How to earn this badge

Make sure that your chosen topic is not covered in any of the Junior badges, and that it does not conflict with the Girl Scout Promise and Law.

Ask your council for approval of your badge topic.

With your leader, talk about why you want this badge and the kinds of activities that will help you and others the most. Then write your own activities on the next page, agree on a name for the badge and a design for the badge symbol. The name of your subject goes in the blank space in the title Our Own Troop's   badge. Each girl puts the badge symbol the troop has designed on her own blank badge with the green border.

Do the activities in a way that is satisfactory to you, your leader, and your consultant (if you have one for this badge).

When you have completed your badge, send a copy of the activities and a sample of the cloth badge you designed to your Girl Scout council office.

Each year the council office sends a list of all the Our Own Troop's badges in the council to the Program Department at Girl Scout national head-quarters. People in both places want to know the kinds of badges you like to do.

Our Own Troop's Badge

_____

_____

_____

_____

_____

_____

_____

_____

_____

_____

_____

My signature

_____

Leader's signature   Date badge completed

Our Own Council's Badge

Some Girl Scout councils have an Our Own Council's badge. Ask your leader to check with your council office to find out if your council has such a badge.

Junior Girl Scout Signs

The four Junior Girl Scout signs were designed to help you explore the variety of activities available to you in Girl Scouting. Three of the signs are described in this book. The fourth one may be found in the **Junior Girl Scout Handbook.**

The requirements for the signs are different from those for a badge. A badge is about one area of interest, while a sign includes several different activities important to every Girl Scout. Like badges, signs have activities to help you get started. To complete some parts of a sign, you will earn one or more badges. **A badge or badge activity can only be used once in doing any of the signs.**

Most girls will earn the Rainbow first, but you do not have to earn the signs in any particular order.

Sign of the Rainbow

What is a rainbow?

Red...for the World of Well-Being

Orange...for the World of Today and Tomorrow

Yellow...for the World of the Out-of-Doors

Blue...for the World of People

Purple...for the World of the Arts

Add green for Girl Scouting and you have a rainbow! The Sign of the Rainbow gives you a full variety of colorful choices and is a symbol of hope for your future. It will give you the fun of finding and following several paths. A girl who wears the Sign of the Rainbow has gained new skills in many ways and is able to work with girls in other troops, particularly Brownie Girl Scouts who are ready for bridging.

Do one activity in each section in any order and complete the personal record when you are finished.

I. Complete five badges for this award — one in each world.

I earned these badges: _____
_____
_____

II. Try three activities in **The Wide World of Girl Guiding and Girl Scouting.**

OR Do three activities in the Girl Scouting Everywhere badge.

Here is what I did: _____
_____
_____

III. Do a service project for a group or person in your community.

OR Do one of these badge activities: Architecture, number 5; Books, number 6; Community Health and Safety, number 9; Do-It-Yourself, number 3; Energy Saver, number 4; Healthy Eating, number 2; Hiker, number 8; Junior Citizen, number 9; On My Way, number 8; Troop Camper, number 7.

Here is the way I gave service: _____

_____

IV. Do an activity in **Careers to Explore for Brownie and Junior Girl Scouts.**

This is the activity I did: _____

OR Talk with someone in your community about her/his job.

This is the career I chose: _____

This is the person I talked with: _____
(Name)

(Job)

Person's Initials: _____   Date: _____

V. Get to know the members of another Girl Scout troop or camp unit or prepare for being a Junior Aide by completing two of these activities:

☐ Show by a real-life situation that you know how to talk to someone new and make her/him feel comfortable. Practice beforehand with a friend or your family.

☐ Make a poster or chart showing ways a good hostess prepares for guests or keep a list of what you did as a hostess when you had a guest in your home, at a troop meeting, or in your camp group.

☐ Teach a person or a group a song, game, or dance; or teach a mechanical, artistic, or outdoor skill. You may use a picture, diagram, chart, model, filmstrip, or cassette to help in the learning.

☐ Tell about an experience or show something to a group in such a way that they are excited, entertained, or inspired.

I did these two activities: _____

Personal Record

Many Girl Scout activities help you in finding out more about yourself and in choosing the values you want to live by. Think about each of the activities you have done this year: badge, troop, or camping activities.

Record the activities below that have helped you in the ways described.

This is an activity that helped me understand myself better: _____

_____

This is what I did: _____

_____

I tried something difficult in this activity: _____

This is what I did: _____

_____

I learned new skills in this activity: _____

This is what I did: _____

_____

I improved my talents in this activity: _____

This is what I did: _____

_____

This activity helped me better understand my values and what's most important to me: _____

_____

This is how I will use what I learned: _____

_____

I showed I was thinking for myself in this activity: _____

This is what I did: _____

_____

This activity helped me better understand the Girl Scout Promise and Law: _____

_____

This is how I will use what I learned: _____

_____

My signature _____

Leader's signature _____   Date Sign of the Rainbow completed

Sign of the Sun

The sun is a symbol of great energy. It provides us with light to see and understand better. Seeing and understanding more are important parts of the Sign of the Sun. Earning this sign helps you see yourself, other peoples, and the world in new ways. Your energies will go into becoming a good leader in your troop and making this year a successful one for the troop.

Do one activity from each section in any order and complete the personal record when you are finished.

I. Complete five new badges for this award. Choose the badges from at least two worlds.

I earned these badges: _____

_____

_____

II. Learn about the location and the activities at the world centers from **The Wide World of Girl Guiding and Girl Scouting.**

OR Complete the Girl Scouting Everywhere badge. (This badge is in addition to the five badges in section I.)

III. There are many ways each Girl Scout can be a leader and provide a real service to her own troop. List three ways and/or times you did each of the following during the year:
- ☐ contributed ideas
- ☐ helped plan activities
- ☐ shared in job responsibilities

Here is what I did: _____

_____

_____

_____

_____

IV. Do an activity in **Careers to Explore for Brownie and Junior Girl Scouts** which takes you to see someone working on a job.

OR With your troop or a group of Girl Scouts, visit a place of work in your community and find out about the jobs there.

Here is what I (we) did: _____

_____

V. To help you become a leader in your troop, do one of the following:
- ☐ Keep troop records for two or more months.
- ☐ Be a patrol or group leader for two or more months.
- ☐ Carry out a special responsibility at a day or resident camp for one or more weeks.
- ☐ Take care of planning and managing the finances for a troop camping weekend.

OR Complete the Business-Wise or Household Whiz badge. (This badge is in addition to the five badges in section I.)

Here is what I did: _____

_____

Personal Record

Girl Scouting can help you understand your own feelings and those of others. Think about the activities and projects you have done this year. Record the activities below that have helped you in the ways described.

In this activity I showed I really cared about something important to me: _____

_____

This is what I did: _____

_____

This activity helped me think in a new way: _____

This is the new way: _____

_____

In this activity I tried something new: _____

Here is what I did: _____

_____

In this activity I listened to and helped others: _____

Here is what I did: _____

_____

In this activity I worked well in a group: _____

Here is what I did: _____

_____

In this activity I found I could express myself more easily to others: _____

_____

This is what I did: _____

_____

This activity helped me to get along with others: _____

Here is how it helped: _____

_____

_____

My signature
_____

Leader's signature   Date Sign of the Sun completed

Sign
of the
Satellite

Satellites were made to view and explore new horizons. They aid communication in many ways. You will be adventuring out into new worlds which are beginning to open up to you. The Sign of the Satellite will guide you into exploring ways to help yourself, your neighbors, and your community.

Complete one activity from each section in any order and complete the personal record when you are finished.

I. Complete three badges for this activity, one from each of the following: the World of Today and Tomorrow, the World of the Arts, the World of the Out-of-Doors.

I earned these badges: _____

_____

II. Work on and participate in a project or event related to worldwide Girl Guiding and Girl Scouting for your council or for one part of the council.

OR Complete the Hands Around the World badge.

OR Participate in a ceremony or event to share Girl Guiding/Girl Scouting with family and friends.

Here is what I did: _____

_____

III. To increase your understanding of young children, families, and homes do one of these badges: Tending Toddlers, Child Care, Home Living.

I earned this badge: _____

Here are some ways I can use what I learned in this badge: _____

_____

OR Spend ten hours or more helping with children. This may be by baby-sitting or helping in a day-care center, day camp, Brownie troop, or playground.

Here is what I did: _____

_____

IV. Do three badge activities for this requirement to learn more about career fields that interest you. These are some examples of badges that have activities you might want to choose:

Architecture, number 6

Boating, number 10

Community Health and Safety, number 6

First Aid, number 9

Hands Around the World, number 1

Horse Lover, number 10

Music Lover, number 6

On My Way, number 9

Putting Things Together, number 1

Science Sleuth, number 7

OR Do three activities for this requirement in one badge that will help you learn more about a career field that interests you.

OR Explore a career of interest to you through **Careers to Explore for Brownie and Junior Girl Scouts.**

Here is what I did: _____

_____

V. To better understand your community and your world do one of these badges: My Community, The World in My Community, Wide World, Eco-Action.

I earned this badge: _____

OR With others in your group or patrol, use the skills you have learned through badges to design and carry out a community action project to show your concern for people in your community.

This is what I (we) did: _____

_____

Personal Record

Girl Scouts and Girl Guides have always made important contributions to their communities. Being a friend and a sister of every other Girl Scout and helping in times of need have been part of these contributions. Think about the activities and projects you have done this year. Record below the activities that have helped you in the ways described.

During this year, I have learned these new things:

☐ about my family _____

_____

☐ about my community _____

_____

☐ about my world _____

_____

During this year, I have:

☐ helped my family in these ways _____

_____

_____

☐ helped to make the world a better place in these ways _____

_____

_____

_____

My signature

Leader's signature   Date Sign of the Satellite completed

Junior Aide Patch

The Junior Aide patch represents active assistance (as a Junior) to Brownies who are bridging.

Many Brownies do not know all about Junior Girl Scouting. When you work on bridging activities with girls in their last year as Brownies, you teach them what to expect and how to make new friends. In addition, it gives you a real chance to use your hospitality and planning skills and to serve sister Girl Scouts.

How-To

If you are in your first or second year as a Junior, look over and discuss with your leader the requirements for a Junior Aide patch.

With help from your leader or council, find a troop of Brownies where girls are bridging.

If you have decided to earn the Junior Aide patch by helping Brownie Girl Scouts in bridging activities, make a plan. For help in making your plan, see the **Junior Girl Scout Handbook.**

Requirements

Do two or more of the following with girls in their last year as Brownies.

1 Using your **Junior Girl Scout Handbook,** help Brownie Girl Scouts select and do an activity from the book.

2 Invite Brownies to a patrol meeting and/or Court of Honor meeting. Explain how the patrol system works. Help Brownies set up a bridging patrol of their own.

3 Visit Brownie meetings and tell the Brownies about Junior Girl Scouting. Teach them songs or games you know or demonstrate camping skills you have learned.

4 Be a buddy to a Brownie who wants to work on a Dabbler badge. Help her get started. If you haven't done the badge, you might start it too.

5 Invite Brownies and their leader to go on an overnight camping trip with your troop or plan a backyard camp-out just for them. Meet with the Brownies and help them learn what they'll need to know.

6 Invite Brownies to help plan and participate in a service project your troop wants to do.

7 Invite Brownies to one of your troop meetings. Let the Brownies ask you any questions they have about being Junior Girl Scouts.

8 Show and tell them about your uniform and badge sash, and talk about things you have done in your troop.

9 Tell Brownie Girl Scouts about the outdoor skills in the **Junior Girl Scout Handbook.** Demonstrate and/or teach them the ones they don't know.

These requirements can be changed or added to, to suit the needs and interests of yourselves and the Brownies you are assisting. There is no "right" or "wrong" way for Brownies to bridge to Juniors, or for you to help them.

My signature

Leader's signature   Date Junior Aide patch completed

Bridge to Cadette Girl Scouts Patch

During your last year as a Junior Girl Scout, before you become a Cadette Girl Scout, you can choose to earn the Bridge to Cadette Girl Scouts patch. The activities for this patch will help you to find out about some of the fun and adventures that await you when you become a Cadette Girl Scout. You must complete at least one activity in each of the following eight steps. Keep track of what you do by filling in the record of your bridging activities in the blank spaces. This patch is also described in the **Junior Girl Scout Handbook.**

BRIDGING STEP 1:
Find Out about Cadette Girl Scouting

☐ Look through the resources for Cadette Girl Scouts — the **Cadette and Senior Girl Scout Handbook, Cadette and Senior Girl Scout Interest Projects,** and **From Dreams to Reality: Career Cards.**

☐ Fill in the "Now I Am" chart on page 21 in the **Cadette and Senior Girl Scout Handbook.**

☐ Find out about the Girl Scout Silver Award.

☐ Find out about the uniforms and recognitions for Cadette Girl Scouts.

☐ Look at **Wider Ops: Girl Scout Wider Opportunities** to find out about opportunities that Cadette Girl Scouts might be qualified for.

☐ Talk with a Cadette or Senior Girl Scout who had been on a wider opportunity.

☐ Find out about the Reader's Digest Foundation Grants for community service.

☐ Invite a girl who is a Cadette to tell you about Cadette Girl Scouting.

☐ Find a Cadette or Senior Girl Scout who can help you with bridging activities.

What I did:_____

_____

_____

What I learned: _____

_____

_____

Date completed: _____

BRIDGING STEP 2:
Do a Cadette Girl Scout Activity

☐ Do an activity from the **Cadette and Senior Girl Scout Handbook.**

☐ Do an activity from **Cadette and Senior Girl Scout Interest Projects.**

☐ Do a career exploration activity found in chapter 6 of the **Cadette and Senior Girl Scout Handbook.**

What I did: _____

_____

_____

Date completed: _____

BRIDGING STEP 3:
Do Something with a Cadette Girl Scout

☐ Be an international pen pal to a girl who is between twelve and fourteen years old.

☐ Go on a field trip.

☐ Learn how to use an outdoor stove.

☐ Do a service project.

☐ Do an art or science project.

☐ Plan a menu for an outdoor camping trip.

☐ Do a flag ceremony.

☐ Work with a Leader-in-Training to plan an activity that will be done with Daisy Girl Scouts.

Name(s) of the Cadette Girl Scout(s) I worked with: _____

_____

_____

What we did together: _____

_____

_____

Date completed: _____

BRIDGING STEP 4:
Share What You Learn about Cadette Girl Scouting with Junior, Brownie, or Daisy Girl Scouts

☐ Teach them something you learned about Cadette Girl Scouting.

☐ Tell them about a field trip or service project that you did with a Cadette Girl Scout.

☐ Tell them about a wider opportunity that a Cadette Girl Scout went on.

☐ Show them pictures of the Cadette Girl Scout uniform and tell them about the recognitions that Cadette Girl Scouts can earn.

Names of the girls I shared information with: _____

_____

_____

What I did: _____

_____

_____

Date completed: _____

BRIDGING STEP 5:
Do Cadette Girl Scout Recognition Activities

☐ Earn a Dabbler interest project patch for one of the worlds of interest, as described in **Cadette and Senior Girl Scout Interest Projects.**

☐ Earn an interest project patch by doing one of the following projects from **Cadette and Senior Girl Scout Interest Projects:** Child Care, Sports, Invitation to the Dance, Hi-Tech Communication, Eco-Action.

☐ Do an interest project activity from each world of interest in **Cadette and Senior Girl Scout Interest Projects.**

☐ Do three activities in chapter 6 from the **Cadette and Senior Girl Scout Handbook.**

What I did:_____

_____

_____

Date completed:_____

BRIDGING STEP 6:
Take on a Leadership Role

☐ Teach safety rules to younger children.

☐ Teach others to make something.

☐ Do activity #1 in the Leadership interest project in **Cadette and Senior Girl Scout Interest Projects.**

☐ Help recruit Girl Scout members for your Girl Scout council.

☐ Earn the Junior Aide patch (see page 201, **Girl Scout Badges and Signs**).

☐ Assist the leader of a group of younger Girl Scouts.

What I did:_____

_____

_____

Date completed:_____

BRIDGING STEP 7:
Help Plan Your Bridging Ceremony

☐ Learn how to do an opening or closing for your ceremony that is different from any opening or closing you have done before.

☐ Do a Girl Scouts' Own ceremony.

☐ Write a special poem about Junior or Cadette Girl Scouting.

☐ Compose a song for your ceremony.

☐ Design and make special invitations for your bridging ceremony.

☐ Make decorations to be used at your bridging ceremony.

What I did: _____

_____

_____

Date completed: _____

What our bridging ceremony was like (when it was, who was invited, and what happened): _____

_____

_____

_____

Date completed: _____

BRIDGING STEP 8:
Plan and Do a Summer Girl Scout Activity

(You may be able to get your Bridge to Cadette Girl Scouts patch before the summer. But, be sure to do this step over the summer.)

☐ Go to a Girl Scout camp. _____

☐ Do a summer service project. _____

☐ Plan an all-day outing with some other Girl Scouts. _____

☐ Plan and hold an outdoor slumber party. _____

☐ Plan and have a campfire. _____

What I (we) did: _____

_____

_____

Date completed: _____

Badges and signs were developed by the following program specialists on the Girl Scout national staff: Carol N. Green ☐ Mabel A. Hammersmith ☐ Carolyn L. Kennedy ☐ Verna Lewis ☐ Lynn Ann London ☐ Elizabeth Munz ☐ Corinne M. Murphy ☐ Nancy H. Richardson.

Badges were also developed by the following consultants: Constance L. Bell ☐ Judy A. Boling ☐ Georgiana Bonds ☐ Edith C. Brown ☐ Lorrie Davis ☐ Kelley House ☐ Roberta Kankus ☐ Sandra Kaufman ☐ Judith S. Kendall ☐ Carol Knapp ☐ Norma Jo McCarrell ☐ Ellen McEvoy-Knights ☐ Dehra W. Shafer ☐ Jean Schaeffer ☐ Dr. Glenn M. Thatcher ☐ Muriel Thatcher ☐ Mary Theresa Webb. Girl Scouts of the U.S.A. wishes to express its gratitude to RCA Corporation for a grant that made possible the participation of eight of these consultants.

Girl Scouts of the U.S.A. also wishes to thank the girls and leaders who field tested the badges, as well as the numerous individuals, including girls, council volunteers and staff members, national staff members, and friends outside Girl Scouting, who contributed ideas and critical review of the badges. Information, technical help, and/or critical review was also provided by representatives of the following agencies and organizations:

Allan and Barbara Anderson: Architects and Planners ☐ American Association for Leisure and Recreation ☐ American Red Cross ☐ Boston (Mass.) Public Schools, Department of Fine Arts ☐ Camp Horsemanship Association ☐ Conservation Consultants, Pennsylvania ☐ The Humane Society of the United States ☐ Information Center on Children's Cultures, U.S. Committee for UNICEF ☐ Museum of American Folk Arts ☐ National Audubon Society ☐ National Marine Education Association ☐ National Sea Grant Program ☐ The Ninety-Nines ☐ North Carolina Bicycle Safety Commission ☐ Northern Michigan University, Department of Chemistry ☐ Orienteering Services, U.S.A. ☐ Society of Women Engineers ☐ United States Coast Guard Academy, Department of Physical and Ocean Sciences ☐ United States Coast Guard, Office of Boating Safety ☐ United States Department of Agriculture ☐ United States Department of Energy ☐ United States Product Safety Commission, Division of Consumer Information ☐ United States Small Business Administration ☐ The University of Arizona, College of Fine Arts ☐ The University of Michigan, School of Natural Resources ☐ The University of Victoria (British Columbia), Department of Biology ☐ Women's Sports Foundation ☐